In the *Midst* of thee

VOLUME 1

STORIES BY

GLENN RAWSON

Acknowledgments

This note is to say thank you to all those who have helped bring these stories to a large and receptive audience. Many thanks goes to my family and friends for letting themselves be exploited. Carl Watkins deserves boundless thanks. These stories were his brain-child, and he has been a guiding hand behind the scenes in every story produced. Thanks to Jeremy Chatelain for his editing expertise. Thanks be to Brian and Rachel Hanson my friends and business partners. They have been there in every venture and have never given up on the vision.

Many thanks goes to those who have listened and encouraged us in presenting these stories. Lastly, thank you to everyone who has let me tell a story about them. They have allowed all the world into their sacred private lives. Their willingness to share has edified many. This book comes in response to numerous requests for the printed stories in a compilation. We offer them now in hopes that they may help someone. Helping someone come closer to God and their family was the sole motivation for these stories in the first place. Thanks be to God for all His gifts and tender mercies.

Glenn Rawson

Contents

Happiness

Once, while serving as a missionary on a very cold Midwest winter morning, my companion and I went out to meet people. In an effort to ward off the cold and discouragement, we began telling jokes to one another. As we approached a stranger's door, he told me a joke, and I didn't get it; went right over my head.

I continued, however, pondering the punch line. Then, just as the door began to open, I got it, and it was hilarious! I started laughing so hard I could hardly talk, as did my friend.

When the lady of the house opened the door, she saw two young men on her doorstep, laughing uproariously! I tried to stifle my mirth long enough to state our purpose for being there. I'm afraid it came out more as a series of garbled snorts and chokings. I don't think to this day she knew what I said but the wonderful thing of it all is that she began laughing also. Soon, we were all having a good laugh. She was still chuckling as she closed the door and sent us on our way.

Life is wonderful, and there is so much to laugh at and enjoy. If we come to the Savior, who was the most cheerful of all men who ever lived, He will teach us how to find the happiness and the joy that was the purpose of our creation in the first place. When the Savior said "be of good cheer" (John 16:33), it was a commandment, not a suggestion.

Robb And Caleb

Sometimes the most powerful of sermons are not what we say; they're what we do.

One day I was sitting in my church services listening to a young man who had just returned from a two year mission in Detroit, Michigan. The first thing that impressed me was how much Robb had grown while he was gone. He'd always been a big young man, a rodeo cowboy, well over six feet tall, with a powerful build. But now, there was a spiritual bigness about Robb. You couldn't see it, but you could feel it.

Robb spoke on the theme of "letting your light shine before men," and he told of touching experiences with young children and elderly ladies. It was a sight to see. More than once, this big, tenderhearted cowboy melted to tears as he spoke of people he had loved and reached out to in Michigan. His sermon was well spoken.

When the meeting was over, the congregation began to sing the closing hymn. A young father, Marcus, stood up to direct the music. His little boy, Caleb, followed him up on the stand. As the song got under way and Dad's arm got into motion, Caleb suddenly decided it was time for adventure and exploration. He began moving farther and farther away from his dad, running back and forth, in and out of, and around the choir seats, having the time of his life. Of course, all of this was to the entertainment of the entire congregation.

From where I was sitting, it was obvious Dad was uncomfortable. At first, he just kept looking over his shoulder to see what Caleb was doing. But, as Caleb got farther out, Dad got more and more nervous. Soon, Marcus stopped singing and then stopped leading altogether. He turned around and motioned for Caleb to come back. Caleb only grinned broadly and ran in the opposite direction. Everyone wondered what Dad was going to do. Junior was making a scene and disrupting the whole meeting. Dad's dilemma was whether he should skip the music, take off and chase the boy down and make it worse, or whether he should let Caleb go and pray that Caleb would settle down.

Without any warning, my big cowboy friend stood up and walked back into the choir seats where Caleb was playing. Caleb saw him coming and started to run, thinking it would be a chase. Robb simply sat down and with a big grin on his face, motioned for Caleb to come to him. Cautiously, Caleb sidled over to Robb, and Robb scooped him up on his lap and began talking to him. To my surprise, Caleb nestled inside those big arms like he had known Robb all his life, and there he stayed for the rest of the meeting.

It's hard to describe how that affected me. I guess being a dad myself, I have a soft spot for those things. In two quiet minutes with a tiny child, Robb taught me more about letting your light so shine before men, than in the entire twenty minutes of his talk. I want to be more like that.

Water-skiing

One cannot truly appreciate the joy of conquering something unless he has painfully failed a few times.

One summer I was invited by some friends to go water-skiing. I had never water-skied in my life, and what's more, I can't even swim. When I get in water over my head, my panic button goes bonkers; I float like a rock. So, I don't know whether it was male ego or a fit of foolishness, but I agreed to go.

When it came my turn, I was given some brief instructions. Bobbing like a cork, I eventually managed to strap those ungainly boards on my feet that, for some reason, were always trying to get above my head. When I was set, I signaled for Wade to hit it. Oh, and he did! I think I drank half the lake before I finally let go of that silly rope.

I rounded up the skis to try again. This time I made it up on the skis, but I couldn't keep a steady pressure on the rope. Wade accelerated to take up the slack when, suddenly, my ski tips caught. The next thing I knew, I was flying through the air superman-style, hanging onto that rope. When I finally hit the water at thirty miles-per-hour, I  had no idea something as soft as water could hurt so much!

I was ready to say, "That's it! That's enough! I'm too old for this much fun." But, when I could finally breathe again, my dad's words from childhood came to me, "When you get bucked off, boy, you get back on!"

It was with some trepidation that I put those boards back on my feet. As I sat there poised to hit it again, I found myself saying, "Heavenly Father, I have to do this. Please help me!"

Wade gunned the boat, and I popped right up, and to my joy, this time I stayed up. And you know, it was fun! I made a couple of passes around the lake until I was comfortable, and then once more, I crashed, rather ingloriously, when I tried crossing the wake. Nonetheless, I had gotten up, and little by little, as the day went on, my skill and my confidence increased until the last time I skied I was glad to finally crash. I had been up so long and skied so many times around the lake, I was too tired to hang on anymore.

Whether it's water-skiing or overcoming the natural man, the principle is the same. We learn to rise above this murky mortal lake of wickedness we live in by painfully crashing into it a few times. No matter how humiliating and embarrassing the wreck, God always comes back for you. Those crashes hurt, but they are necessary and expected. How else can we learn? If we will grit our teeth, pray hard, and try again, we will rise above it until someday we will, by the grace of God, become skilled enough to stay above it.

Watch The Lamb

The apostle John made a statement within a statement in the book of Revelation, "Worthy is the lamb that was slain."

Nearly two thousand years ago, the Jews of Jesus' day commemorated the Passover, that sacred event from their history when the angel of death passed over them, while all the firstborn among the Egyptians died.

On Thursday, sometime in the late afternoon, Peter and John, at the Savior's command, took a lamb and, under the direction of the priests in the temple, killed it and spilled its blood. They then prepared the Passover for Jesus and the rest of the twelve. That evening, He and they came to partake of the last officially authorized paschal lamb.

Four thousand years God's people had been sacrificing the lambs and shedding their blood as an offering for sin. Even now, thousands of lambs would be killed over two days time.

The thought of such a thing, and especially as part of my religious devotions, seems distasteful and disgusting. Why would God have commanded such a thing of them?

I don't know all the reasons. But as I studied it and thought about it, I learned some interesting things. The lamb was a symbol to point them to the time when their Redeemer would come and be the final offering. For example, consider some of the following:

Each of those lambs selected was male, unblemished and perfect, just as Jesus would be.

Each was innocent, undeserving of its fate, just as Jesus would be.

Each was meekly submissive, just as Jesus would be.

Each was brought by the head of the household to be sacrificed on behalf of the family, just as Jesus would be.

Each had its blood forcefully shed and thus its life taken, just as Jesus would.

Each was sacrificed in the holy place, just as Jesus would be in the holy city.

Each Passover lamb was sacrificed under the authority of Israel's priests, just as Jesus would be.

Each was sacrificed without a bone broken, just as Jesus would be. Each lamb was of the first year, cut off in the bloom of life, just as Jesus would be.

And, each had another's sins placed upon it and vicariously died, just as Jesus would.

After the shedding of great drops of atoning blood in Gethsemane, Jesus is led away like a lamb to Golgotha, where, on Friday morning, He is lifted up and sacrificed. For some six hours, He hangs in indescribable agony. Then, sometime around three o'clock in the afternoon, perhaps even while the paschal lambs are dying in the temple, Jesus dies, the ultimate offering for the sins of the world. In His offering, I have part. Because of it, I am encircled in the arms of mercy. No more were the lambs to die. It was not necessary. The horrible price was paid. Man was free!

For many years, I was tempted to rail and accuse those who missed the significance of the lambs and their blood when it was fulfilled, until it occurred to me—unless and until I understand the significance of the bread and the wine, I had better be quiet. May the Lord bless us to more fully watch the lamb and understand the offering made for us.

Elijah

Elijah from the Old Testament was considered the prophet of the prophets. And yet, during his ministry, an event occurred from which great strength can be drawn in tough times.

Elijah labored with his whole soul to bring the nation of Israel unto Jehovah, even calling down incredible displays of divine power to persuade the people. Still, he was rejected and hated by the very people he came to save.

Running for his life, Elijah fled into the wilderness, where he made a most interesting request of the Lord. He said, "It is enough; now, O Lord, take away my life; for I am not better than my fathers." It was a plea as if from a very burdened and discouraged prophet.

In the spirit of fasting and prayer, Elijah went deeper into the wilderness, all the way to Sinai, where the word of the Lord came to him and asked, "[Elijah,] what doest thou here?"

In response, Elijah poured out his soul to God.

Notably, when Elijah finished, God did not pity him or commiserate. What good would it do? Instead, He brought Elijah to the mount, and there began an awesome display of the powers of nature: wind, earthquake, and fire. However, the record says God was not in them, meaning, Elijah was impressed but still discouraged.

Then there came a "still small voice" from God, the voice of His Spirit, and Elijah was healed. It spoke peace to his wounded, burdened heart. The result, Elijah got up and went back to work with renewed zeal.

Is it hard sometimes to swim in the deep waters of mortality? Is there a tendency at times to want to give up? Is the Lord angry with us on those days when we just can't go on, when we just can't do it anymore? No! Especially not when we're trying to be good. The still small voice that spoke peace to Elijah is as much ours to claim, as it was his, if in our prayers we reach deeper than trite phrases and get to where the heart really is.

See 1 Kings 19:4-14.

Close Enough

There are some problems that arise in our lives that are just beyond the scope of our ability to solve. I think a wise and loving Heavenly Father has made sure of that. Why? Well, if we could solve every problem, answer every question, and cope with every crisis ourselves, what need would we have of Him? There is a much better world than this one waiting for those who, in their extremity, reach out for His power.

Thronged by a crowd, Jesus followed the anxious Jairus on an errand to heal his dying daughter. Within that crowd was a woman afflicted with an incurable disease. In seeking a cure, she has spent all her fortune. Now, still not healed, she is more sick than ever.

Somehow, she learns of the Great Healer and determines to go to Him, but because of the nature of her illness, she is ashamed to ask for His help.

As Jesus passes in the crowd with Jairus, she says to herself, "If I may but touch [the hem of] his garment, I shall be whole" (Matthew 9:21).

She pushes her way through the crowd, and from behind, she touches the Master's robe. Immediately, there is a tangible surge of power that flows throughout the woman's body. She is fully healed from that very moment!

Filled with emotion and gratitude, she drops back into the crowd, out of sight. Jesus, however, stops, turns around and scans the crowd.

"Who touched me?" He asks.

In essence, Peter says to Him, "There are all these people pushing and shoving, and you ask, 'who touched me?'"

Jesus makes it clear, though, that this touch was different than any other. "I perceive," says He, "that virtue [power] is gone out of me."

The woman, knowing she was discovered, comes forward, falls at His feet, and confesses what she has done. With kindness and tenderness, the Master commends her for her faith.

"Daughter," He says, "thy faith hath made thee whole; go in peace" (Luke 8:45-48).

This woman felt unworthy of Him, yet she compelled herself forward, driven by an overwhelming sense that she simply had nowhere else to go. That is how we exercise faith. We push ourselves toward Him, especially when we don't feel like it. And now, as then, there will come power into our lives, the power to heal, the power to change, but only—only if we will come close enough to touch.

See Matthew 9:20-22, Mark 5:25-34, and Luke 8:43-48

Drusilla Hendricks

We admire our pioneer ancestors for their courage and their sacrifice. We read about what they did and stand back in awe, wondering if we could do the same these days.

In 1839, Drusilla was living in the happiest days of her life—a new home, a new faith, and a loving family. Then one night her world was changed. Her husband, James, was shot in the neck by a mob, leaving him paralyzed from the neck down. The mob then drove her from her home and ransacked it. The family returned to their home only to be ordered to leave the state immediately.

Drusilla sold the family land for enough money to buy oxen to pull a small wagon, and then set out for Illinois in the cold, winter weather of early March. When she finally settled, friends built a log cabin for her, which she then chinked and plastered herself.

To make ends meet, Drusilla, with a family of five children under the age of eleven, began raising a large garden, taking in boarders, and selling homemade gingerbread and mittens. Drusilla worked hard; she did all she could to support herself.

As before, their peace was only temporary. Mobs descended upon her people, and in the winter of 1846, Drusilla again loaded up her family, crossed the Mississippi River, and turned her face to the West.

They had not gone far, however, when word came that volunteers were needed to join the United States Army in a war with Mexico. By now, Drusilla's oldest son, William, was eighteen, and William wanted to join the army. For seven years this son had been her greatest help. There was no way. How could she give him up? How in the world would she survive a more than one thousand mile journey across the wilderness without him? There was no way.

One morning, as Drusilla was preparing to fix breakfast, the familiar voice of the spirit spoke to her in words such as these:

"Drusilla, do you desire the greatest glory of heaven?"

"Yes, Lord," she answered.

"Then, how can you get it without making sacrifices?"

"Lord, what lack I yet?"

The voice of the Lord came softly, "Let your son join the battalion."

William joined the army with his mother's urging. However, the pain and the grief were too much for her. Seeking seclusion, Drusilla knelt down and poured out her heart, as only a mother would understand, to a loving God. She told the Lord He could take her oldest son if He wanted, "but please, please Lord, spare his life."

With the "peace that passeth all understanding," the Lord spoke to this woman of awesome faith. Gently and reassuringly, He said, "It shall be done unto you as it was unto Abraham when he offered Isaac on the altar."

True religion requires sacrifice or it will never produce strong faith. We, of this pampered generation, need not worry about whose sacrifices were greater, the pioneers' or ours. For the faithful, a just and loving Father in Heaven will make sure the sacrifices and trials we endure are sufficient for the glory we will receive. Those of us who are fond of our comfort and ease must realize there is a price to be paid for faith.

It was once said this way, "No cross, no crown; No gall, no glory; No thorns, no throne" (Ezra Taft Benson, Area Conference Report, Taipei, Taiwan, 1975, p. 3).

See Historical Sketch of James Hendricks and Drusilla Dorris Hendricks. Typescript: LDS Church Archives.

The Palsied Man And His Friends

It seems these days, when I kneel down to pray, the faces of a lot of people I care about who are in trouble come to my mind. A lot of my time in prayer is spent for them, hoping beyond hope that Heavenly Father will bless them because of my meager faith and my much concern.

But, do you sometimes find yourself wondering if it's doing any good? Will He really help them just because you ask Him to? Is He really listening? Are your feeble efforts with them and with Him making any difference at all?

On one of those rare occasions when the Master was at home in Capernaum, word spread quickly throughout the community that He was there, and a crowd came together. So large a crowd, His house filled to overflowing. To those close enough to hear, which evidently was not all, Jesus taught the Gospel.

Four men approached the house carrying a sort of portable bed, upon which lay a man who was paralyzed. They tried to enter the house and get to Jesus, but they could not for sake of the crowd. Selflessly determined, these four men hefted their helpless friend up onto the flat roof of the house, and removed part of the roof. After creating a hole, they lowered their friend through the hole right into the middle of the crowd near Jesus. With compassion, Jesus bade the man to be of good cheer, forgave his sins, and healed his paralysis.

Mark's words were, "When Jesus saw their faith..." (Mark 2:5). Notice it's not "his faith," but "their faith."

In other words, here was a man in the spiritual bondage of sin and the physical bondage of paralysis, who is healed in part by his own faith, but in great measure by the faith and determination of those who loved him and were willing to sacrifice for him.

The next time you wonder if your pitiful prayers are doing any good, please remember this statement from the apostle Paul, "The effectual fervent prayer of a righteous man availeth much" (James 5:16). And so it does.

See Matthew 9:2-7, Mark 2:1-5, and Luke 5:18-20.

When You Believe

Are there times when your faith and belief just aren't quite what you'd like it to be? Maybe there's something you need to believe in.

How much more could one young woman's life be shattered than was Mary's at that moment? The final days of her senior year in high school should have been filled with joy, excitement, and anticipation of the future. In an instant, that changed.

Mary came home from school as usual that day. Her parents gathered the family around the table for a grim announcement; Mother had cancer!

Mary cried herself to sleep that night.

A few days later, the family was again gathered around the table, the results of the most recent tests were even more devastating. The cancer had spread throughout her body.

Hiding her emotions, Mary prepared dinner for the family and got ready to go to work. Just before she went out the door, she stopped and gave her mother a hug.

Four years before, Mary's mother had battled cancer and won. With the simple faith of a pure child, Mary had asked God to save her mother's life, and He had answered that prayer. But would He now? There was no such assurance, though there had been many, many heartrending prayers.

Mary climbed into the car to go to work. Difficult questions raced through her mind. What if Mother died? What would the family do? What would she do? How could she go on without her mother? It was too much to bear. Mary began to cry. In an effort to direct her thoughts elsewhere, Mary turned on the radio.

As she listened, she recognized the final chorus of a familiar popular song. The words captured her attention, and she listened until the song ended. Mary switched stations. Strangely enough, the exact same song was just beginning on the other station. This time as Mary listened, the power of the song reached deep into her heart. She heard these lyrics, "Now we are not afraid, even though we have much to fear."

Something not of this world began to envelop Mary. "It felt as though Heavenly Father put His arms around me," she said. "I fell into His arms."

Her feelings overwhelmed her. "I can't do this!" She cried.

A sense of intense love and comfort that could only be described as a heavenly embrace filled her whole being. A voice seemed to speak to her mind saying, "Mary, don't be afraid. I'll be with you the whole way. Trust me. I only want what's best for you." Her tears of pain became cleansing tears of relief.

Words from the second verse seemed to strike a resounding chord in her heart, "With hearts so full I can't explain." The expressions of the artists were the emotions of her heart.

A change came over Mary from that moment forward. She is at peace. What's going to happen? She doesn't know, but it doesn't matter. No matter what it is, life will go on. There will be happiness, there will be joy, and she won't be alone. That she does know!

Eighteen months later, Mary's mother quietly passed away surrounded by her family. It was not the miracle Mary had hoped for, but she outlived the doctors' predictions, even recovering just long enough to nurse Mary through her own health crisis.

God is good! He will not do anything to us that is not for our good. So what good could possibly come of such an ordeal? Listen to the courage of Mary's words, "No matter what life may give me, I know if I have total trust in God, everything will be okay. I'm not alone, and I will never stop believing."

> *"There can be miracles when you believe.*
> *Though hope is frail, it's hard to kill.*
> *Who knows what miracles you can achieve*
> *When you believe? Some how you will.*
> *Now you will; you will when you believe."*

Michelle Pfeiffer, Sally Dworsky, "When You Believe,".

Nicknames

Jesus is our Savior. But, if all there was to His being our Savior was His redeeming sacrifice, then the Savior's work ended nearly 2000 years ago. I want you to know that such is not the case; His redeeming work is not done. He is still involved in our lives. One of the reasons Jesus is our Savior is because of His ability to see the divine in each one of us that we cannot, and through His love, bring it out.

Consider John, chapter one when the Savior first meets Simon Peter. Andrew brings Simon to meet the Savior. When the Savior sees him, He says to him, "Thou art Simon the son of Jona: thou shalt be called Cephas," or Peter in the Greek, "which is by interpretation, [a seer or] a stone" (John 1:42).

Can you imagine what those words must have done to Peter? One minute you are Simon, a lowly Galilean fisherman, and the next, you are a fisher of men, a personal friend of the Messiah, a seer, the greatest calling a man can have, and a man of rock! Surely, Peter would never have forgotten those words. Like a beacon before His soul, He would follow them and spend the rest of His life living up to them.

Furthermore, look at the nickname the Master gave two others of His apostles, James and John. He called them "Boanerges," which means "The sons of thunder" (Mark 3:17).

We all have things about ourselves we want to change. I have found, and so have you, it is so much easier to change when we have a friend to help us. The Savior is that friend. From the first moment we begin to become acquainted with Him, we feel the gentle but firm upward tug of His love and faith. He will not rest until He has drawn forth from us every talent, every virtue, and every power lying latent within us that we will give Him. And so it is.

Teaching, A Sacred Trust

One summer I was hired by a neighbor to tend a small band of sheep. My job was to take them to the mountain pastures each day, watch them, and then bring them safely home each night. I had been strictly warned when I took the job, not to let the sheep stray too near the alfalfa fields, or they'd break through and bloat on the rich feed.

One day, I carelessly let the sheep get too near the fence and they broke through. The entire band quickly spread across the field and began gorging themselves. I panicked. I ran around screaming and waving my arms desperately trying to drive the sheep out, but it did no good at all. They melted around me like water and went on eating.

Finally, the owner and his son came. As they hurried past me to save the sheep, one of them said something to me about the instructions I had ignored. It angered me, and in a rage I turned and ran, not toward the sheep, but away from them. I ran all the way home. At that moment, I couldn't have cared less if every last one of those sheep had died. Fortunately, though, none of them did.

The experience has come back to me often. I've since learned that a teacher is a shepherd. Teaching is the Savior's own profession. It is the art of shepherding the lambs of God to the pastures of truth, whether that pasture is religion, science, mathematics, or whatever. Truth is truth, no matter where it's found! And, teaching, is a sacred trust.

Speaking as a father, may God bless those teachers who will touch the lives of the children. Someday, teachers, who's to say how grateful those lambs will be for you and for all those who guided them safely to pasture and brought them back home?

Kidney Stones

One night after a late night family movie, my little boy, Adam, crawled in bed with me, wanting a bedtime story. I was just a few pages into "Beauty and the Beast" when, suddenly, a pain hit me in the back and began to intensify. Within moments, it was so bad I couldn't breath. When I sat up, it felt as though someone had stuck a knife in my back. I knew what it was; I'd heard of it before, kidney stones.

My wife and daughters got me to the hospital, and I have to tell you, I've known pain in my life, but I have never known pain like that! The hospital hooked me up to IV's and began to pump me full of painkillers. Oh, they were wonderful! I still remember the feeling. One of the painkillers was called Tordal.

However, if I had known what this drug would do to me, I would never have gotten within a hundred yards of it. While I languished in the hospital, the kidney stone refused to move. So, the hospital naturally increased the fluid drip into my body in an attempt to flush the stone out. I don't know how many bottles of that stuff went into me.

By late Sunday night, the stone was still there, as was the pain, and something was definitely wrong with my body. None of the fluid going in was coming out. The Tordal had shut down my kidneys. By the time I left the hospital for home, I resembled the Pillsbury Dough Boy, and the stone was still there!

The words "retaining water" took on a completely new meaning. None of my clothes would fit. It was so bad that even sweat pants were tight. I lost sight of my feet for the first time in my life; I couldn't even bend over. For the next several days, whenever I lay down to sleep, I felt as though I was being hung upside down. When I climbed on the scales, I discovered that in my thirty-six hours in the hospital I had gained over thirty pounds, and I only normally weigh one hundred fifty pounds dripping wet!

At one point, I came downstairs utterly appalled at my awful appearance. I said to my wife and my oldest daughter, "Look at this!"

I pulled up my sweatshirt and grabbed my more-than-ample stomach and shook it! It jiggled and rolled like a giant bowl of unset jell-o. It was disgusting! They thought it was hilarious; they still do.

My wife, having borne seven children, made some comment in the midst of her gales of laughter like, "Well, now you know what pregnancy feels like, don't you?" I don't recall I ever really wanted to know what pregnancy felt like.

I went to my doctor, who's a good friend. He was a little surprised at what had happened to me; I guess Tordal was not supposed to do that. He said, "Well, we need to get your kidneys going again."

He gave me some pills and, oh, did they work! Over the next four days, I lost all of the thirty pounds plus more, underwent surgery for the stone, and painfully passed two more stones. When it was over, my body felt like it had spent a week in a washer on the spin cycle!

The lesson? Knowledge is power. What we don't know can hurt us, just like what I didn't know hurt me. Our agency is only as good as our knowledge. The more we know of truth, the stronger our agency, the more choices we have, and thus, the more power we have over our lives. What we don't know limits our ability to choose and allows us to be deceived.

If only I had known that my troubles could likely have been prevented by a few extra ounces of water each day. Likewise, most of our troubles in life can be solved by a few extra minutes of living water, the Word of the Lord studied and applied.

Experience taught me that taking Tordal and guzzling IV fluid has terrible consequences. If only I had known. Don't let experience teach you about guilt, pain, and hell. Remember, knowledge is power. Ignorance and stupidity are not bliss, they're bondage! May we stand in the light of the Lord Jesus Christ and never be moved.

Rachel And Adrian

I remember a line from a movie produced years ago that had a powerful, even a life-changing impact on me. The line was, "No one can make it happily through this life and into the next without the Savior."

I've thought about that line. How do we go out and lay hold upon the kind of happiness spoken of in a world so full of opposition? Why, also, is it that the most seasoned and mature of the Savior's disciples are the ones who love life the most, when they are often the ones bearing the most difficult burdens?

Rachel first met Adrian in October of 1994, on a blind date. They spent a wonderful weekend together with sparks flying while attending church meetings. There was something about this young man who loved the Lord so much that interested her. Their next date was again to a sacred church experience. By December, the interest between the two of them had transformed into an eternal love. On Christmas Eve, Adrian gave Rachel a significantly wrapped Christmas gift. Rachel opened it, and inside was a book entitled "Just For Newly-Weds." It was his proposal—what a way to ask!

They were married in June of 1995, excited at the prospects of beginning a whole new life together. Two years later, they graduated from college. Adrian enrolled in a Master's program in Physical Therapy. One year after they were married, Mason came along adding a sweeter dimension to their marriage. Three years after that, Carter was born.

"Adrian was the greatest dad," Rachel said. "He was always playing with his boys, wrestling, basketball, tickling them." Rachel described coming home on more than one occasion and finding Adrian on the sofa curled up with Mason in his arms, both of them taking a nap together. Life was wonderful.

After two long years, Adrian's graduation neared. He was excited to begin work as a physical therapist. It was about this time he noticed a nagging pain in his side. Doctors initially diagnosed it as gastritis, but the pain didn't go away.

The day after Adrian finished school, he woke up very sick. This time Rachel knew something was terribly wrong. The doctor called them in, pulled his chair right up next to them, and announced "Cancer, pancreatic cancer." They gave him a five percent chance of survival. "They never gave us any hope," Rachel said.

Within two weeks, Adrian underwent radical surgery. He recovered, but never completely. Over the next ten months, Adrian deteriorated steadily, until he was little more than an emaciated shell.

Those ten months were in some ways glorious. It was just Adrian, Rachel, Mason, and Carter all day, everyday, together as a family. There were many late night talks between Adrian and Rachel planning and preparing for the future—how to raise the boys after he was gone.

Then one morning, Rachel awoke, and Adrian was gone. It was Easter morning.

Some would say it was cruel and unfair to leave Rachel, a twenty-six-year-old widow, with two little boys to raise alone. Not if you ask her. She's not alone. There is something about this young woman, an infectious cheerfulness and optimism that radiates from her like a light. When I asked her about it, she said it was her goal to be happy, to be pleasant.

"I want Adrian," she said "to look down and see me happy."

How could anyone be happy and cheerful under such trying circumstances? I believe I found the answer when I went to her home. There are several pictures hanging prominently around the family room, mostly photographs of the family, including Adrian. However, there is one portrait occupying the central place in the room. It is of the Lord Jesus Christ, He who once said, "I am the way, the truth, and the life" (John 14:6). "He that believeth in me, though he were dead, yet shall he live" (John 11:25). This is what makes Rachel the way she is.

Faith is not just to believe in Christ, that He's out there, somewhere. It is to believe Christ, that He will be there, that He will keep His promises to us. When we believe in Christ in this way, it is called faith. When faith is there, hope is born within us beckoning us to follow Him, counting on His promises. Such hope is now an anchoring force holding Rachel and her boys steady and serine on the straight and narrow path.

Not long ago, their little boy Mason offered this prayer: "Heavenly Father, please help Daddy to be happy in Heaven. We're thankful the Gospel is so true, and that we can be a family forever if we live so righteously."

To be hopeless is to be homeless. Look at your life. If your hope has dimmed or disappeared, come unto Christ as a little child and find it again. Life can be glorious in spite of it all.

Prayer

Richard L. Evans once said, "He who ceases to pray loses a great friendship."

Like all friendships, even ours with our Heavenly Father takes time and effort on our part to develop. It doesn't come naturally. Misunderstandings must be corrected, and doubt and laziness must be overcome.

As a small child, Annie shared a room with her sister. Each night as they would go to bed, she would either make sure she said her prayers first, or she would wait until her sister was finished. In her childlike innocence, she believed if she and her sister were praying at the same time, Heavenly Father would get confused, wouldn't understand, or would ignore her entirely. She wanted His full and undivided attention.

Since then, my friend has come to understand she always has His undivided attention.

In her own words, "I still don't know how He can be aware of us all, hear us all, and know us all at the same time, but I know He can."

Trust The Pilot

A couple of years ago, my wife and I flew with a pilot friend of ours and his wife to Sun Valley for a dinner date. Our plan was to fly over and come back that night. It was my first flight in a small, single-engine aircraft, and my friend had only had his license a couple of months.

The view was magnificent as we returned that night, high above the Arco desert. It seemed as though we could see forever in all directions, and the stars overhead were beautiful. Even now, it's difficult to describe what it was like.

As we approached our hometown, Jerry, the pilot, commented he couldn't see the airport runway marker lights in the darkness. His comment brought all of us to full attention. The chatter in the cockpit was instantly silenced, replaced by a keen sense of fear and nervous tension; we were scared!

We approached and circled the town, but the lights were nowhere to be seen. We would have to land in the dark.

It didn't seem to me, at the time, that I had a lot of options. I could panic and become a screaming idiot, I could take over the controls of the airplane, or I could open the door and jump out. None of the options seemed very appealing. For the first time in recent memory, I considered that I might die.

Then, Jerry looked at me, and with a calm confident demeanor said, "Don't worry. Trust me."

Something in what he said, and the way he said it, spoke peace to me, and I was no longer afraid; I felt calm.

Jerry circled and brought the plane down where he thought the runway should be. In spite of my assurance, it was still a tense moment watching the blackness of the earth rush toward us. It turned out we were slightly east of the runway as the plane's lights hit the ground. Although, with a quick skillful maneuver, the plane's course was corrected, and we landed without mishap. I don't know if I have ever been so grateful to put my feet back on the earth.

Later, I reflected on the experience. It seems our lives are like that plane flight. We are all flying in a darkened world, and it's too late to turn back. We're in the air; we're committed. The only choice we have is to see the flight through to the end. When we get ourselves into trouble, as we all do, some of us are tempted to quit, to bail out, and end it all. Others of us arrogantly take over the controls. Both solutions have the same eternal consequence, misery and further pain.

There is a better way, one that will bring peace and happiness, and leaves us free to enjoy the experience and the incredible views that will be opened to us.

That solution is simple. Trust the pilot. Let him take over the controls, and not only will we arrive at our Heavenly destination, but by the grace of God, we will have had a grand and glorious adventure.

Tom

Sometimes what we most need in this difficult world is a friend, someone whose encouragement is constant, who won't coddle us, but won't let us be beaten up either.

It was a warm summer afternoon. Tom was out on the back patio of his Las Vegas home, when he heard shouting and angry voices from inside the house. As he entered, he saw one of his teenage sons pitting his stubborn will against the determined correction of his mother. Tom's desire was to calm the situation and reconcile his loved ones. But, within minutes he was drawn into the conflict, shouting worse than the other two. It wasn't long before mother and son stormed out in opposite directions, leaving Tom standing there.

He felt terrible. He returned to the patio; shame and guilt washed over him. He had only wanted to help, but instead he'd made the

situation worse. Right there on the patio, Tom knelt down and began to pray—praying for forgiveness, acknowledging his pride and his unbecoming behavior, and asking that peace and a healing spirit be poured out upon his wife and son.

And then it happened. It was as clear as if it were audibly spoken. A voice out of eternity echoed in Tom's mind. "Father, Tom has done it again! But he wants to do good. For Me, please grant the petitions of his prayer."

Tom said, "I marveled. It was so personal. With countless people on the earth, the Father and the Savior were attentive to me in that moment. I knew with certainty the Master had somehow reached into that infinite reserve He had earned in Gethsemane and paid the price unalterable justice required. And I was free of pain of heart."

The sense of forgiveness was real and soothing for Tom. Within a few minutes, the same spirit moved upon his wife and son. They came together; apologies were shared, and a healing was affected. Harmony and peace were restored once more to their home.

Our Savior is our advocate and our truest of friends. If we will let Him, He will not only stand between us and justice, but also between us and a world seeking to bully and destroy us. Even our own weaknesses and fears will eventually give way to the power of our omnipotent friend. Thank God for the gift of His son, the gift of the truest of friends.

C. S. Lewis

I don't think it would be too bold to say that more rumors, legends, and traditions have been perpetuated about the Savior of the world than any modern celebrity ever dreamed of. Every conceivable notion has been advanced to explain who He was and what He was. I have lost track, according to supermarket tabloids, how many times His second coming has occurred. The more things change, the more things stay the same.

Sometime in the second year of the Savior's ministry, Jesus and His apostles went off alone. As they went, Jesus asked them, "Whom do men say that I the Son of Man am?"

The apostles answered according to the rumors circulating among the people at the time, "Some say that thou art John the Baptist: some, Elias; and others, Jeremias, or one of the prophets."

Rumor had it among the Jews that Jesus was John the Baptist come back to life after being killed by Herod. Even Herod believed it. Still, others believed Jesus was Elijah the great prophet, taken to Heaven without tasting death, whom the scriptures promised would return before the great and dreadful day of the Lord. And still others superstitiously believed Jesus was Jeremias or another of the prophets reincarnated. It seems rumors are always more popular than the truth.

Then Jesus asked them, "But whom say ye that I am? And Simon Peter answered and said, Thou art the Christ, the Son of the living God."

Peter had received revelation from God, and so must we. Until we do, until we know what Peter knew, Jesus' identity and importance will always remain a matter of doubt to us, and a source of weakness. For a doubting and cynical world, perhaps the great Christian philosopher C. S. Lewis put it best. He said:

> I am trying here to prevent anyone saying the really foolish thing that people often say about Him: [That is] 'I'm ready to accept Jesus as a great moral teacher, but I don't accept His claim to be God.' That is the one thing we must not say.

A man who was merely a man and said the sort of things Jesus said would not be a great moral teacher. He would either be a lunatic – on a level with the man who says he is a poached egg – or else he would be the devil of Hell. You must make your choice. Either this man was, and is, the son of God; or else a madman or something worse. You can shut him up for a fool, you can spit at him and kill him as a demon; or you can fall at His feet and call Him Lord and God. But let us not come with any patronizing nonsense about His being a great human teacher. He has not left that open to us. He did not intend to.

See Matthew 16:13-16.
See also C.S. Lewis, Mere Christianity, New York: Macmillan Publishing Co., 1952, pp. 40-41.

The Vision Of Enoch

The earth has approximately six billion people on it. Has it ever crossed your mind how in the world can God keep track of all of us? Not to mention loving us and hearing us? Moses recorded a touching story from the life of Enoch the prophet, valuable for all of us.

After Enoch built his remarkable city called Zion, he received a vision in which he saw Zion eventually taken up into heaven, leaving behind those people who, for the most part, had not chosen righteousness. Enoch is then permitted to see nation after nation of these people, some of whom repent and are saved, but most going on in wickedness. Then Enoch sees Satan laughing with a great chain in his hand, veiling the whole face of the earth in darkness.

Immediately following the vision, he sees an interesting thing, Enoch sees God weeping. He is evidently surprised and asks, "How is it that the heavens weep, and shed forth their tears as rain upon the mountains...How is it that thou canst weep, seeing thou art holy, and from all eternity to all eternity? And were it possible that man could number the particles of the earth, yea, millions of earths like this, it would not be a beginning to the number of thy creations; and thy curtains are stretched out still; and yet thou art there, and thy bosom is there; and also thou art just; thou art merciful and kind forever" (Moses 7:29-30).

Even in the asking, Enoch's question is an incredible revelation. With an infinity of worlds and children, the God of the universe for us is here; His heart is here, His tears are here, and He is merciful and kind forever. When God's children suffer, no matter where they are, especially if it's unnecessary, He suffers with them, even to tears.

There may be nearly six billion people on this earth, but that's okay. When you know the eye of God is upon you, and the heart and soul of God are with you, it no longer matters how many others there are, or where they are, it becomes as though you were the only one.

See Moses 7.

Mitchie

I am convinced we are not alone in this world. There is a loving power who knows us, who watches over us, and guides us if we'll listen.

A few months ago, my brother-in-law had an experience which, even now while telling, fills his eyes with tears and his heart with deep gratitude.

Late one night, well after his children were all down in bed, he made his way to his second floor bedroom. As he passed the top of the stairs, he noticed a light on downstairs in the kitchen. Knowing the family was in bed and all the lights should be off, he paused. Puzzled, he asked his wife if she had left any lights on. She answered that she hadn't. He contemplated the long journey down the stairs to turn it off. Fatigue won, and he decided to leave it on and go to bed.

Turning toward his bedroom, he was stopped by a gentle impression to investigate. He nearly ignored it, sleep was calling more loudly, but the feeling persisted.

Without doubting further, he descended the stairs. As he rounded the corner into the kitchen, he discovered Mitchie, his two-year-old son up on the kitchen counter, surrounded by the contents of two containers of high potency medicine. Both caps were off, and a bright pink ring circled the toddler's mouth. Reacting quickly, he rushed the boy to the hospital, where competent medical personnel acted swiftly and saved his life.

You will never convince Shayne he wasn't prompted by the God of Heaven, not ever so long as he can look into the bright vibrant eyes of that beloved son, who will evermore serve as a reminder of the goodness of God.

Life Isn't Fair

Not too long ago, on a beautiful spring day, I came home from work and found two of my daughters playing in the front yard. One of them didn't look very happy. I invited her to sit down with me on the front step and asked her what was wrong. She launched into a tirade, as only a five-year-old can, about how everything is so unfair and so hard, especially at kindergarten.

Oh, it was bad! The teacher had criticized her work, she couldn't sit with her favorite friend, her sister wouldn't play with her, her brother wouldn't wrestle with her, and on and on she went. She was having a bad day, and there was nothing I was going to say that was going to change that.

Well, I got an idea. Since I couldn't reason with her to help her feel better, maybe I could distract her.

"Look, Honey," I said, pointing to the sun that was just going down, "the sun's going behind the tree. Ah, now I won't get to see it anymore; I won't get to feel its warmth anymore. That is so unfair!"

She looked at me funny, and said, "No, it's not!"

"Yes, it is," I argued. "Now I'll never get to see it again!"

"Yes, you will."

"No, I won't."

We argued back and forth, I, pointing out the unfairness of the sun going down, and she, promising its return.

Finally, with great earnestness and some exasperation, she blurted out, "It's okay, Dad! The sun will come out again!"

I stopped, and looked at her expectantly for a moment. But she didn't get it. Maybe she never will. Yes, she will, someday.

I smiled at her, and we went out for ice cream.

Whitewashed

In our daily struggle to overcome the big sins, it often helps to remember the little ones, too. For example, where would we be if God got offended as often as some of us do?

Some time ago, I was with a group of young friends. After several hours of intense meetings, we decided to get out of the cabin and have a good old-fashioned football game, girls and all. There we were, a dozen or so people bundled to the hilt in winter clothing in a tackle football game in several feet of snow. I was by far the old man of the group, but I joined in. On one of the first plays, I caught a pass and was instantly knocked off my feet into a snowdrift. They had no mercy for the old man.

As the game went on, the competition was fierce and the hits were hard. The girls in the group tackled as hard as they got tackled. I'm sure all of us got our chimes rung a few times, but no one complained, and we had a good time. The most notable thing to me was that no matter how hard they got hit or whitewashed in the snow, no one got angry, not even close.

At the conclusion of the game, we began walking back to the cabin, tired and cold. One of the guys, still feeling rambunctious, tackled one of the girls, and, in spite of her protests, buried her face deep in the snow. She came up spitting and sputtering! I thought she was going to hit him. He jumped up laughing and went after another girl, and similarly whitewashed her.

Just a few minutes later, one of the guys had stripped off all of his snow clothes and was standing on the porch in socks, gym shorts, and a tee shirt. Along came our problem child and shoved him out into the deep snow, forcing him to do the cold-toe-two-step.

I watched all this with keen interest to see how my three wronged friends would react. Would they get offended? To my surprise and delight, none of the three got angry, despite more-than-sufficient provocation. I watched closely as each of them made a decision to shake off not only the snow, but the anger. They chose to laugh, and they went on and forgot it.

In spite of fourteen hours together, in cramped quarters, with intense interaction, we were better friends at the end of the day than at the beginning. Why? Because of a lot of laughing, and no offense was taken.

Being offended is natural, but that's just it. It is of the natural man, not the divine man. If we want to, and by the grace of God, we may become quick to laugh, slow to anger, and a light unto the world. After all, it's like what my grandmother used to say, "Getting offended is like getting a head cold. It just makes snots out of people."

Daddy

The Psalmist said, "Children are an heritage of the Lord" and "Happy is the man that hath [many] of them" (Psalm 127:3, 5).

Not long ago, I was sitting in a church meeting with my four-year-old daughter on my lap. The congregation was singing. Not terribly interested in singing, she became fascinated with my pocket hymnal, which has my name embossed on the front.

She reached up, grabbed my head and pulled it down where she could speak in my ear.

"Daddy, whose name is that?"

"Well, that's my name, Honey. See," I said whispering, "Glenn Rawson."

My daughter is very matter-of-fact and minces no words.

"That's not your name!" She said.

"It's not?"

"No!"

Suddenly, I was very curious to know who my daughter thought I was. So I asked, "Well, then what is my name?"

She didn't even hesitate. "It's Daddy!"

It's hard to describe how her words tugged on my heartstrings, but it did. Still, I felt she ought to know all daddies have other names too. So I said, "Well, that's true, Honey, but I also have another name. It's Glenn Raw…"

"No!" She said firmly. "Your name is Daddy!"

I gave up trying to change her mind. I just smiled and hugged her. Since that time, the name "Daddy" has become more special to me. My hope is, as time goes on, she never becomes too old to think of me as her "Daddy."

The Weeping Woman

No one can truly love the Savior and know Him if they've never needed him.

Early in the Savior's ministry, He was invited to the house of Simon the Pharisee, who seems, even in his invitation, motivated by an arrogant curiosity about the Master. Simon disdainfully neglects the usual social customs afforded an honored guest.

During the course of the meal, while guests recline feet-outwards on couches around the table, a woman enters and stands at the feet of the Savior. Without a word, she falls at His feet weeping and begins kissing His feet, bathing them with her tears, and wiping them with her hair.

Simon, knowing something of the woman's sinful reputation, scorns the Master in His thoughts and watches the proceedings with contempt. Discerning those sin-darkened thoughts, Jesus defends the woman's actions and rebukes the self-righteous, judgmental Pharisee. With penetrating clarity, the Savior taught, "To whom little is forgiven, the same loveth little."

To the penitent, grateful woman, and with tender mercy, the Master declares, "Thy sins are forgiven...Thy faith hath saved thee; go in peace." When our love and faith in the Savior of the world drives us weeping to our knees, seeking His power to forgive, we, too, can then come to truly love Him and know something of the joy of "mercy's arms."

See Luke 7:36-50.

Orange Juice

One Sunday afternoon, we were just finishing our family dinner when, somehow, the conversation turned to popular movies. One of my daughters mentioned a very popular movie that had one of those objectionable scenes in it.

She said something like this, "Dad, what's so wrong with that movie? I'd really like to see it. We can always fast forward that two minute part."

She knew about the bad part in the movie. She knew it was wrong, but the rest of the movie had captured her imagination, and she wanted to see it.

Instead of arguing with my daughter, I remembered something a friend of mine had done in a class. Sitting on the table was a pitcher of orange juice with just one cup left in the bottom. I poured the last cup, held it up, and asked her if she wanted it. My children love O. J., and, of course, she wanted it.

"Okay then," I said, "follow me."

With most of my children curiously following, I took the glass of orange juice and walked into the bathroom. I reached into the toilet with another cup and dipped out some toilet water. Ever so carefully, I poured just one tiny drop of toilet water into the orange juice.

I held it out to her. "Here you go," I said.

She screamed and ran out of the bathroom.

"But, honey," I said as I held it out to her, "it's only one little drop."

"I don't care!" She yelled. "It's yucky!"

You know, I could not get her to come within ten feet of that glass of orange juice. I finally had to pour it out.

Since that time, I have not had a single argument with any of my children about which movies they should be watching. I hope I never have to.

The prophet, Isaiah, once said, "Be ye clean, that bear the vessels of the Lord" (Isaiah 52:11). To my way of thinking, it is time! For the covenant people, it is time!

The Marathon

Family and family relationships are as vital to complete and lasting happiness as water is to an ocean.

Not too long ago, I decided on my next birthday I would run a marathon. I don't know why, I just wanted to see if I could do it. I had no desire to run a formally organized marathon, I wanted to do this all by myself, just to see if I could. It was then I discovered it was just the right distance to run from my front door to the LDS Temple, a little over twenty-six miles. Perfect!

At 4:45 a.m., on the appointed day, all stretched out and ready to go, I left my house and started running. The first 13 miles went quite smoothly, but about mile eighteen I hit "the wall!" My legs felt like lead. It felt as though my feet were one big hypersensitive nerve, and my toenails were being torn off. I seriously began to wonder if I could make it to the end.

I'd only had about a month and a half to train for this marathon. During that time, I watched my children get excited about my goal. Sometimes they even went running with me. If I stopped now, how would I face them and explain my failure? I couldn't. I pushed on. I have never felt such concentrated, intense pain, especially self-inflicted.

As I ran, I kept promising myself I would stop and rest when I reached this or that goal, but for some reason when I reached the goal, I kept going. Around mile twenty-five, moving slowly, but still moving, my family drove past me hollering and screaming on their way to the Temple. I was so glad I was still running.

At one point, just a couple blocks from the Temple, I was stopped by traffic. Not even a goal is worth getting run over! When I finally got across the street and tried to run again, I couldn't. I couldn't make my legs work, it hurt too much!

Then, more staggering than running, I rounded the last corner and saw my family standing at the Temple's southwest corner with a ribbon stretched across the sidewalk. At that same moment, I heard my son shout, "C'mon Dad!"

It's hard to describe how those words hit me. They went deeper into me than he'll ever know in this life. I was overwhelmed with a feeling of love and gratitude for my family.

Suddenly, this marathon became something more than a feeble man's goal. It became something eternal; it became a microcosm of life. I saw my wonderful little family standing on the soil of eternity, cheering me on as I struggled to endure the pain of finishing the most grueling race I had ever run—the race against myself. Sobbing and gasping for air, I crossed their little tape with not even enough strength to pull it out of their hands. Instantly, they surrounded me, hugging and congratulating me. My exhaustion was so complete, I couldn't even talk. The crowning moment came when they pinned a gaudy little homemade ribbon on my chest that said, "Number One Dad."

The marathon of a righteous mortality will be the toughest experience we will ever face as eternal beings. A wise and knowing Father knew it would be, and thus gave us a fan club, people to support us and cheer us on, a family. I believe as we strive to faithfully finish life's race, we are loved, watched, and cheered on by family on both sides of the veil. When our race is run and we finally cross that line, we will gratefully fall into the arms of an anxious and loving family with whom we are "number one." Who would ever want to go into eternity without their family?

State Trooper

What kind of father is God? How does He work with His children? What's His "style of discipline," if you will?

Not long ago, I was driving along a busy Idaho highway in a tractor-trailer. It was a beautiful morning, and I was thoroughly enjoying it. Part of that particular highway is posted with a fifty-five mile-per-hour speed limit. The other part is sixty-five. I thought I was on the sixty-five mile-per-hour part. I wasn't, but was driving like I was. Down the road I went, clipping along, taking in the scenery, enjoying the day, and just loving life, when suddenly I passed an Idaho State Trooper. I didn't give him much thought. I mean, why should I? I was legal—wasn't I? No sooner had I passed him than my CB radio came to life, causing me to jump.

"Hey, Handy," a deep voice said.

"Yes," I answered.

"You're going sixty-nine miles-per-hour."

I laughed nervously, "Yes." I knew who it was.

And then he said, with kind of a drawl, "Do you have an extra $53 you don't know what to do with?"

"No," I said, "I'll keep it."

"Fifty-five miles-per-hour will do just fine," he said firmly.

"Okay, thank you."

You could almost see the grin on this officer's face as he added, "You owe me."

"That I do," I said, "that I do." I went on my way down the road, relieved and chuckling to myself. I obeyed that speed limit for the rest of the day.

The patrolman could have really taken it to me. He had every right. I was clearly in the wrong; I was breaking the law. He could have pulled me over, chewed me out, inspected my rig, cited me, and done a host of other things if he'd wanted to. But he didn't, and at least for my case, he didn't have to; it wasn't necessary. I'm pretty conscientious about obeying traffic laws. All I needed was a gentle reminder.

We are not perfect. All of us break the laws of God. If God wanted to, He could be harsh, really harsh! But He's not that way. For those of us who are trying, He doesn't need to. His style of discipline doesn't perform radical surgery when a hug and a band-aid will do just fine. He's kind, He's gentle, and He's persistently persuasive with reminders. In fact, a line from a hymn comes to mind, and to me it says everything about the parenting style of Heavenly Father. It says, "How gentle God's commands! How kind His precepts are" (LDS Hymn #125)!

The Christmas Story

There are no stories told that will have near as much power on the human heart as the words of the scriptures themselves. One such example is the "Christmas Story."

"And it came to pass in those days, that there went out a decree from Caesar Augustus, that all the world should be taxed. (And this taxing was first made when Cyrenius was governor of Syria.) And all went to be taxed, every one into his own city. And Joseph also went up from Galilee, out of the city of Nazareth into Judaea, unto the city of David, which is called Bethlehem; (because he was of the house and lineage of David:) To be taxed with Mary his espoused wife, being great with child (Luke 2:1-5).

"And so it was, that, while they were there, the days were accomplished that she should be delivered. And she brought forth her firstborn son, and wrapped him in swaddling clothes, and laid him in a manger; because there was no room for them in the inn (Luke 2:6-7).

"And there were in the same country shepherds abiding in the field, keeping watch over their flock by night. And, lo, the angel of the Lord came upon them, and the glory of the Lord shone round about them: and they were sore afraid. And the angel said unto them, Fear not: for, behold, I bring you good tidings of great joy, which shall be to all people. For unto you is born this day in the city of David a Saviour, which is Christ the Lord. And this shall be a sign unto you; Ye shall find the babe wrapped in swaddling clothes, lying in a manger. And suddenly there was with the angel a multitude of the heavenly host praising God, saying, Glory to God in the highest, and on earth peace, good will toward men (Luke 2:8-14).

"And it came to pass, as the angels were gone away from them into heaven, the shepherds said one to another, Let us now go even unto Bethlehem, and see this thing which is come to pass, which the Lord hath made known unto us. And they came with haste, and found Mary, and Joseph, and the babe lying in a manger. And when they had seen it, they made known abroad the saying, which was told them concerning this child" (Luke 2:15-17).

To The Teachers

It seems a traveler, in the eastern country, overtook an old gentleman one day, walking towards a town, and asked him, "Who's the great man of that little town? Who's your leading man? Who's the governor and controlling spirit of that little place?"

The old gentleman replied, "I am the king of that little town."

"Really!" Says the traveler. "Are you the leading man?"

"Yes, sir. I am king in that place, and reign as king."

"Well, how do you make this to appear? Are you in affluent circumstances?"

"No, I am poor. But in that little village there are so many children. All those children go to my school. I rule the children, and they rule the parents. And that makes me king."

Even though I'm a teacher, I'm also a dad. As a father, I would say to those "kings" who teach the children, my children:

Teacher, please teach the truth, pure, unadulterated, diamond truth.

Teacher, you are not better than your student, and the student has been taught to trust you.

Teacher, what you are speaks louder than what you teach. Long after your students have forgotten the precepts you taught, they will remember how they felt when they were with you.

Teacher, your students are under attack by destructive forces on all sides. Please, never weaken their armour.

Teacher, this world is full of the unseemly and perverse. May the domain of your classroom be a haven of light and empowering truth.

Teacher, when you enter the heart of the child, you stand on sacred ground. Tread carefully, for surely someday you will be accountable to a greater father than I.

Teacher, the children are hungry. Nourish them with truth and feed them well.

Teacher, my children are mine before they are yours. In all you say and do, please strengthen the bonds of my family. Never, please, never weaken it.

Teacher, you will have many in your charge, sometimes too many. Please don't forget your greatest impact will likely be one on one.

Teacher, you hold great influence with your students, and well you should, but remember, you do not need personal disciples.

Teacher, it's a turbulent world out there. I hope your classroom will be a sanctuary where those children are safe.

Teacher, you have the awesome power and ability to open their minds. Very well, open them and open them wide. But when you leave them, may it never be with doubt and error, but always truth and hope.

Teacher, the world these children are entering is tough, unforgiving, and competitive. Don't coddle them. Stretch them, work them, and teach them to love learning. They will be forever grateful.

Teacher, there is so much of ill manners and crudity in their environment. Please teach them manners and discipline them in their use.

Teacher, they won't always have you. I hope you will teach them to discover truth on their own and value it. Remember, what you are making of the children is not a graduate, it's a citizen.

Teacher, please speak plainly. Don't attempt to dazzle them with your brilliant intellect. Teach them in such a way that they cannot possibly misunderstand the truth.

I know most of you teachers cannot speak of the God you love in your classroom, but you can speak to God about them, about your students. You can bind them to Him by your prayers and faith, and thereby call down His blessings on them. That may be the greatest thing you ever do for them. That may be your greatest demonstration of love.

God bless you noble teachers. We love you; we count on you; may you ever have a burning sense of the trust that has been placed in you by the fathers here and the Father hereafter. Thank you.

Hannah And The Movie

It was Easter Sunday. My family was watching a movie on television entitled "The Lamb of God," about the life and Atonement of the Savior. I left the room for a moment, and when I returned, I found my eight-year-old daughter down on the floor, curled up hiding her eyes and crying.

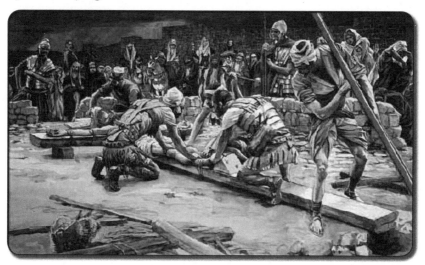

"It's scary!" She said. "I don't want to watch it."

I looked at the screen. The Savior was stretched out on the ground, and the big Roman hammer had just driven the nails into His hands. I picked her up off the floor and cradled her on my lap. She snuggled in tight, and I explained what was happening and why as we watched Jesus be lifted up on the cross and die. I told her how Jesus suffered as payment for our sins and our mistakes so we wouldn't have to.

The scenes changed to the morning of the resurrection. I narrated the movie as Mary came to the tomb and found it empty, and as Peter and John ran to see for themselves. I explained the significance of

John standing alone in the empty tomb and turning back to look one more time. He believed!

I really wanted Hannah to understand. Yes, it is a scary movie, but it has the happiest ending of all time.

After the movie was over, I was standing alone in the kitchen thinking, wondering if she really did understand. If ever there was a question for the ages, it has to be, "why was it necessary that Jesus suffer and die in such a horrible way?" And, if ever there was anything absolutely vital to understand, it's the Atonement of Christ.

I called her to me, knelt down on her level, and asked, "Hannah, why did Jesus have to die in such a scary way?"

She looked at me and said, "Well, so that when we make sin, we don't get in so much trouble." The answer was classic.

The Psalmist said, "Out of the mouths of babes...thou hast perfected praise" (Matthew 21:16; Psalms 8:2). In her simple and profound way she was absolutely correct! Because of Him, we don't have to get in so much trouble. He indeed paid a scary price for our sins. Why? So that we might repent. For if we do not, our sins will be paid for twice, once by Him and again by the unrepentant, and both in the most scary way imaginable!

As for my beautiful daughter, I smiled and gave her a hug. For now, she understands enough.

The Battle
Has Begun

Late one fall evening, after Heber and Vilate Kimball had retired to their bed, they were awakened suddenly by a sharp knocking at their door. A neighbor, John Greene, stood at the door and bade them come out and see the incredible scenery in the heavens.

They did so. It was a beautiful, starlit New England night, so exceptionally clear and brilliant, Heber said later he could have seen to pick up a pin.

As the little group watched, a white smoke or cloud formed on the eastern horizon and slowly began to rise upward. It formed itself into a belt spreading across the sky toward the southwest and was accompanied by the sound of a rushing mighty wind.

Gradually, the belt flattened out and broadened across into a bow, like a rainbow, becoming transparent with a bluish cast, and stretching from horizon to horizon.

No sooner had the bow formed than an army of men appeared, arising from the east and began marching, twelve abreast, across the bow toward the west. As vivid and real as men in the flesh, they marched in the most profound order, every man stepping in the tracks of his leader in perfect synchronization. They were dressed in the full battle gear of 19th century soldiers with muskets and bayonets. They were so clear and distinct, Heber and the small group of neighbors could distinguish the features of their faces and hear the jingle of their equipage as they moved.

Shortly, the entire bow from horizon to horizon was crowded and filled with marching men, the sound of marching reaching clearly to the ears of the astonished onlookers.

Heber later described the event this way, "No man could judge of my feelings when I beheld that army of men, as plainly as ever I saw armies of men in the flesh; it seemed as though every hair of my head was alive."

When the celestial army reached the western horizon, they were met by an opposing force, and a battle ensued. The noise of the rush of men and the clash of the arms was distinct and unmistakable. Heber and his friends looked upon this scene for hours, until finally it gradually disappeared.

Heber's wife, somewhat afraid, turned to one of the older men in the group and asked, "Father Young, what does all this mean?"

"Why, it's one of the signs of the coming of the Son of Man," he replied.

Indeed it was, even though the world missed it, and, just as surely as the meridian world missed the birth of Christ. For you see, that momentous night marked the commencement of the marvelous work and wonder spoken of by Isaiah. It was the same night the angel Moroni delivered the plates of the Book of Mormon into the hands of the prophet Joseph Smith, September 22, 1827.

The battle between good and evil has begun. Welcome to the war!

See Whitney, Orson F., Life of Heber C. Kimball: An Apostle – The Father and Founder of the British Mission, 2nd ed., Salt Lake City: Bookcraft, 1945, p.16-17.

Contention

Not long ago, it was one of those days around my house where everyone seemed to be grouchy and grumpy with "glass egos" everywhere. Snipping and snapping like a cage of sharks, we started our day, and I have to admit, I was no better than the rest of them.

Two of my daughters got into a heated argument over who got to read the new book. The older one grabbed the book from the other, whereupon the younger one grabbed it back and kicked her in the shins!

They managed to work it out, but it troubled me, it really troubled me! As I went to work that day, I was thinking, "What is all this arguing and fighting going to do to my family?" I decided I wanted to say something. I wanted to teach them, but what could I say that wouldn't sound like the drone of a parent's lecture, "You should do this; you should do that; yah, yah, yah..."

I already knew that approach would be just about as effective as getting a kiss through a screen door. So I sat, and I pondered, and then all of a sudden an idea came to me.

That night, I gathered all my family around the kitchen table. I opened up the scriptures and read the words of the Savior, "For verily, verily I say unto you, he that hath the spirit of contention is not of me, but is of the devil, who is the father of contention, and he stirreth up the hearts of men to contend with anger, one with another" (3 Nephi 11:29).

I read the verse, and just as I'd expected, they saw exactly what was coming. They knew perfectly well fighting and arguing were wrong. It was also apparent, once I was done talking, they would remember what I had said about like we remember every mile marker post along side the freeway, and that just wasn't good enough. Somehow, I had to find a way to turn this message into a colossal billboard. Call it a feeling, but it was important to me. This is what I did.

While they watched, I took a photograph of our family, all smiling and happy, and laid it on the kitchen table right in front of them. Then I took an eyedropper with some bleach in it.

"Guys," I said, not telling them what was in it, "this is contention, and this is what it does to our family."

I placed a tiny drop on one of the daughters who had been fighting that morning. Then I dropped another drop on another family member. "Let's just see what fighting and arguing will do to our family." With that, I dropped drops here, there, and everywhere until the whole family was covered.

All of us crowded around and looked down at the picture to see what would happen. I didn't even know; I'd never done this before. Suddenly, right before our eyes, the image of my oldest daughter disappeared from the photograph, then another, and another, until the entire family was gone.

I looked up at my children and said, "Now, what did contention do to our family?"

I can still see in my mind's eye the stunned, awestruck look on my oldest daughter's face as she looked up at me and she said, "It dissolved it!"

And so it does. No matter what the circumstance, contention is never worth it; it tears the family apart! Our families are our joy, not only here, but hereafter. As for me, God's most heavenly heaven would still be hell if the dear ones of my heart were not there. It may take many reminders, and it may take much self-discipline to conquer contention, but I tell you, it is worth it. It is worth it if we can all grow into old age as families, as each other's best friends.

Katie's Prayer

When we pray and expect spectacular and grand answers, we miss the way our Heavenly Father most frequently answers our prayers.

For three years, Katie and her family lived in Argentina. At that time, Katie was a tiny, bubbly, eight-year-old the Argentines affectionately referred to as "la petisa," which means "the petite one."

A necessary part of the family's experience was the dreaded Gama Globulin shot, which they had to receive every three months.

When it came Katie's turn for her shot, she said to her mother, "Mother, I just can't do it. It hurts so much."

Mom tried to reason with Katie explaining to her how vital the shot was for the protection of her health.

"I know, Mommy, I know," Katie said. "I don't want to be sick, but I don't want to get the shot."

Mom looked at her lovingly and said, "It's okay, sweetheart. Go to bed tonight; I'll put the syringe in the refrigerator and we'll talk about it again tomorrow."

Katie went to bed, as did Mom and Dad. A short time later, as Dad finished his personal prayers, he noticed his wife was gone.

When she returned, she had a strange look on her face. "You'll never believe what I just did," she said.

"What did you do?"

"Well, as I was praying, I had the impression that I should give Katie her shot while she was asleep. I got up, went downstairs, got everything ready, and went quietly into Katie's bedroom. There she was with her arm exposed outside the sheet, and I thought to myself, 'what a terrible mother I am!'

I gave Katie the shot, and she didn't budge. Can you imagine me doing something that terrible?"

The next morning, Mom confessed to Katie, "Katie, you'll never believe what I did last night."

"What, Mommy?" Katie asked with a surprised look.

"Last night, while you were asleep, I gave you your shot."

For a moment, Katie looked at her mother in disbelief and then began to cry.

"Oh, Mommy," she said, "last night I prayed that I could get my shot, but that it wouldn't hurt. Mommy, I didn't even feel it."

The Rock Of Offense

Not long ago, I got really curious, and I looked up "rock" and "stone" in the topical guide of my scriptures. I learned some interesting things.

First, I learned Christ was often referred to as the "Rock of Salvation" and "the only sure foundation of righteousness." That seemed a fitting metaphor because, like a rock, He's strong, firm, unchanging, and enduring—capable of weathering the storms and bearing our weight.

Second, I noticed when the Lord and His people entered into covenant relationships, there were usually stones piled or fitted in the form of altars or pillars, which served as continual reminders of those covenants and how they should be as enduring and unchanging as the stones themselves.

Why is it then, given all these qualities about Jehovah, that God's people, over the last six thousand years, have so frequently fallen into apostasy and been destroyed? I found the answer to that question the hard way, literally!

In an effort one day to teach some young people this principle about Christ, the Rock, I brought in to my classroom a huge square lava rock probably weighing about two hundred pounds. Using the rock, I explained that because of the nature of this type of stone, its strength and durability, it was often used years ago to build foundations for homes. We then discussed how the Savior was like the stone, sure and solid, unchanging, able to be the foundation for our eternal house of faith.

However, I explained, for those who will not trust the Savior and follow Him, He becomes a continual nuisance. He becomes the stone in your path on a dark night that causes you to stumble, or worse yet, falls on you and crushes you when you least expect it. The Savior is the stone that will not go away and cannot be avoided.

Well, I used the rock throughout the day to make my point. Looking back, I think it went well.

Late that night, after teaching an evening class, I turned off the lights and strode quickly toward the exit of my classroom. Suddenly, something caught both my shins, causing me to stumble and fall headlong to the floor. I had forgotten my rock. I lay there wounded and bleeding in intense pain, wishing, oh, wishing I had remembered. It took weeks for that to heal.

Just like ancient Israel, I had forgotten Him who must not be forgotten nor ignored. I hadn't meant to. I just forgot!

The Psalmist once said, "Hear my cry, O God; attend unto my prayer. From the end of the earth will I cry unto thee, when my heart is overwhelmed: lead me to the rock that is higher than I" (Psalms 61:1-2).

MaryAnn's Race

MaryAnn saw the truck a split second before the impact. Her next recollection was of hearing someone calling her name. Opening her eyes, she looked down and saw her legs grotesquely broken and bowed. The incredible force of the collision had driven the van's dashboard into the front seats and into her legs, breaking her left leg in a dozen places and snapping the bone in her right thigh.

Rescuers extricated MaryAnn by cutting off her door and her seatbelt. As she was loaded into the ambulance, her legs throbbed with a strange feeling of pressure, and the pain was increasing. Every bump in the road sent bolts of pain through her body.

Within minutes, she was at the hospital, where after extensive X-rays, surgeons installed metal rods in both legs that ran from hip to knee.

MaryAnn had been an athlete, a competitive swimmer, with hopes of one day making it to the Olympics. In 1998, against some sixty other swimmers, she won the local swim-a-thon with a time of 1 hour, 29 minutes and 30 seconds. Her next goal had been to win again and beat her time. "But now?" She wondered.

The day after the accident, with the help of two people and a walker, MaryAnn attempted to stand up, but the pain was so intense she nearly fainted. Thus began one of the greatest challenges of her young life.

The next day, she managed three steps and eighteen inches. The pain was nearly unbearable. After six days in the hospital, she went home. It took three people fifteen minutes just to get her into the car. Again, she felt every bump in the road.

With the daily help of a physical therapist, MaryAnn progressed from walking six feet, to ten feet, and then forty. When she finally went back to school, it was in a wheelchair, then a walker, then crutches, and then one crutch.

One month after the accident, MaryAnn returned to the water only to discover the metal rods in her legs threw off her balance. Moreover, she was unable to kick her feet or push off the wall. She would have to learn to swim all over again.

The day of the swim-a-thon approached. Winning was out of the question. But, should she at least enter and try to finish? Could she? Several people warned her not to try, fearing she would hurt herself. Some even thought she was joking. With a determination as hard as the steel in her crippled legs, MaryAnn resolved to enter the race and at least finish it.

The day of the race came. MaryAnn was still in therapy, unable to walk or run without a limp or even jump off the ground. MaryAnn got into the pool to race. Two hundred lengths and some three miles later, the whistle blew. MaryAnn had won. Her time: 1 hour, 29 minutes, 30 seconds—exactly the same time as the year before.

For those of us that have tried and failed, the Master said, "With faith, all things are possible." If our personal goals are worthy and important to us, then they are important to Him, and He will help us. Just as important to know though, is this. Our pain and sacrifices in obtaining those goals are as critical to our growth as the victories themselves.

The Curb

I learned, when I was a young kid, it is difficult to get a horse to go in a direction he isn't looking, which is why, so critical, a horse must learn to neck-rein. You see, if the horse will go where I point him, he's useful. It not, well, you get the idea. Perhaps it's the same with us; where you look is where you go.

One evening years ago, a friend and I were returning from an appointment, just about sunset. We were traveling down one of the busiest streets in West Des Moines, Iowa, on bicycles. In order to get onto our street, we had to cross the oncoming lanes of traffic. I could see a car coming up ahead, but I had plenty of time. I made the turn, no problem. But, my friend was too close to the oncoming car to make the turn, but tried anyway. He sped up and darted across in front of the car.

As he's doing all these shenanigans, I was looking back over my shoulder. As I pedaled along watching him, I held my breath. I thought for a moment he was going to be a hood ornament with a smile and a suit on, but he made it.

When I looked back around, my bicycle had drifted up against the curb. With all my will power I wanted that bike to go back out in the street where it was safe. In my panic, all I could stare at was the big ugly curb that was coming for me.

Well, it got me! The bike hit the curb and went out from under me. I flew through the air landing on my back and sliding in the slimy wet green grass. My suit I had just gotten back from the cleaners was a mess, and my pride was worse.

I learned from that experience that wherever I'm looking, that is where my bike, my car, or my life will go. If my mind and my heart, my ears and my eyes are constantly filled with, and looking at the distracting and destructive things of this world, is it any wonder I'm continually crashing and unhappy and that my life is a mess?

If we would follow Jesus, then follow him! Fill your homes, your hearts, and most of all, your daily vision with Him, and only Him. Let your eye be single. Then someday, from where He is, we will see as we are seen and know as we are known.

Easter And Rachel

One fall day, several years ago, while sitting in a Spanish class, a friend of mine, Rachel, was paged to the principal's office. As she entered, she was instructed to go to the home of her grandparents—immediately. Feeling confused, she retrieved her books and left. When she got to the house, she went inside and sat down in a rocking chair. Her grandmother sat on the couch nearby. It was obvious she had been crying, but she said nothing. A moment later, Rachel's grandfather walked into the room, placed his hand upon her shoulder and said, "Rachel, your dad was killed in a car accident this morning."

Rachel said, "I felt as if I had been punched in the chest. Breathing was difficult. I sat there in shock as the tears rolled down my face, and I attempted to make sense of what I had been told. How could he be gone? He would no longer be there to answer my math questions, to take me to scary movies my mom refused to see with him, to take me skiing, to promise me that in high school, boys would realize I was alive, and to take me on daddy-daughter dates. He wouldn't be at my graduation from high school or at my wedding. He wouldn't be there to see me go on my first date." And then she concludes, "The pain of this loss continues to this day."

It was a few years later that I became acquainted with Rachel. One day, I could see she was struggling. I invited her into my office to talk, along with a friend. She sat there, more or less stone-faced, refusing to say anything. I knew she was hurting, and I had a pretty good idea I knew why. I persisted in trying to get her to open up and share her feelings. Finally, in something of an emotional explosion, she blurted out amidst her tears, "I miss my dad!" And she began to sob.

I'm not ashamed to tell you those words seared my soul and opened my eyes. I will never forget them. I had no idea what to say to her.

Eventually, Rachel and her family worked through their pain and are courageously learning to cope, as have others afflicted with so great a tragedy.

Now this is why I tell you this tragic, but yet unconcluded story; it's Easter. Nearly two thousand years ago today, on a hallowed Sunday morning, the Lord Jesus Christ took up His body and left the tomb. He, whose body had been completely destroyed, whose heart had been stilled and broken on the cross of Calvary, came forth from the tomb in glorious, living reality.

Yet, there is more to the story. Matthew records the following, "And the graves [of the saints] were opened; and many bodies of the saints which slept arose, and came out of the graves after His resurrection, and went into the holy city, and appeared unto many" (Matthew 27:52-53).

Rachel's story is yet unconcluded, because there will come a day when, like those ancient saints, her father will come forth from the tomb to live again in the flesh. The time away will have only made his love for her and for his family increase.

And the reunion? Well, that's the conclusion of the story. I assure you, for them and for those who keep the faith, the joy of the future will brilliantly overshadow the pain and losses of the past. This is Easter to me!

Get Back On

There is a danger in taking some things for granted. I learned this lesson a few years ago, when I was asked by a friend to break a horse. I was excited. It had been a long time, and I was eager to do it again. I loaded my family and drove over to see him.

The horse turned out to be a large, three-year-old Appaloosa gelding. I climbed through the fence, and he came right up to me. I was under the impression I was only supposed to finish him off, that he was already mostly trained. He seemed really gentle, so I saddled and bridled him right there in the pasture and swung up on his back.

However, when I began trying to neck rein and line him out, all he would do was fight me. The harder he fought me, the more determined I became he wasn't going to get away with it. He was going to do things my way, or else. It didn't occur to me at the time that he didn't have a clue what I wanted of him.

Finally, in frustration, the horse threw his head in the air and reared up. He went higher and higher until he lost his balance and went completely over backwards. It caught me so off guard I didn't react like I'd been taught; I didn't get away from him in time, and he came right down on top of me.

Well, to make a long and embarrassing story short, I was hurt, and it took a long time to get over it.

It wasn't until later that I found out the horse wasn't broke at all. He really didn't know anything. Needless to say, from that day on, I handled him much more carefully; I never again took him for granted.

As I learned to respect what he was capable of, I was able to control him and train him to be a decent saddle horse. All in all, it turned out to be a great experience.

Life is a lot like a large horse. If we get overconfident and reckless, and don't treat it carefully and cautiously, it may wind up sitting on our chest. There we'll be, lying on the ground spiritually torn, bleeding and gasping for air. Life can be dangerous; handle it with care, prayer, and Christ.

Oh, and just in case you wondering, I did get back up, and I did get back on.

Reflections On A Ski Trip

Sometimes the most commonplace of people and events can teach the most profound lessons, if you look carefully.

Recently, I took my three oldest children and went cross-country skiing. At the beginning of our adventure, the four of us encountered a very steep hill. Now, we're all beginning skiers. So while three of us were gingerly inching our way down the hill, my ten-year-old daughter, who seems to have no fear, suddenly came flying past us, digging in her poles for all the speed she could get. She stayed upright all the way to the bottom of the hill, until her skis went tip first into a drift, and she biffed it right in the drift. Sputtering and covered in snow, she came up laughing; I was laughing too. From the top of the hill I thought, "why not?" So I cut it loose. I made it all the way to the bottom too, and then landed in a pile right next to her.

Lesson number one, sometimes in life we are a little too timid. We need to trust the Lord and throw ourselves into life and relationships. So what if we crash once in a while? The fun was worth it.

Later, the weather on our ski trip turned into a blizzard. I had promised the children, when we found the warming cabin at the top of the trail, we'd have hot chocolate and candy for a feast. Our trek toward the cabin became very difficult, so they began to chant, "Hot chocolate, cabin, candy; hot chocolate, cabin, candy," over and over as loud as they could. Eventually, we got all the way up to where we thought the cabin should be, and then we couldn't find it. It was a discouraging moment. We had to turn around and start back without the fire, without the candy, and without the hot chocolate. And you know, there was not one word of whining. What good would it do?

Lesson number two, sometimes we have to be our own best cheerleader. The world is full of whining, sour-faced, pickle suckers. We don't have to be one of them. Life is really a lot of fun if you think about it.

Well, we trudged along, falling frequently, until we came to another steep drop-off. At this point, my oldest daughter was first to go. She made it about ten feet and went face first right into the snow. She came up cold, wet, and sputtering. I heard her mutter as she got up, "I skied up it; I'll ski down it." She got up, went just a short distance, and down she went again. This time, as she got up, I heard her say, "Well, at least I'm getting good at picking myself up." When she was upright, she repeated, this time through clenched teeth, "I skied up it; I'll ski down it." She did too, all the way to the bottom.

Lesson number three, we all need to get good at picking ourselves up. Life certainly has a way of knocking us down, and sometimes frequently. Similarly, God's way isn't always the easiest way, but it certainly is the most thrilling. Don't take your skis off; don't give up, just because the hill gets steep.

Finally, at one point during our trip, my younger daughter took off her skis, and the bindings became iced; she couldn't get them back on. When I came on the scene, I found my son standing in several feet of snow with bare hands and a pocketknife, trying to get his sister on her way. He was cold and wet. He could have skied on by, went right on down the hill, but he didn't.

Lesson number four, I hope he never does. Stopping to help is exactly what his Savior would do.

In conclusion, all things considered, the skiing conditions were lousy that day, but the learning conditions were excellent.

Isaiah 53

There are certain chapters in the scriptures so powerful as they stand, to add any commentary seems only to detract from the power and the sweetness of their message. To me, Isaiah 53, about the life and the atonement of Jesus Christ, is one of these kinds of chapters. If you wouldn't mind, may I share it with you?

"Who hath believed our report? and to whom is the arm of the Lord revealed?

"For he shall grow up before him as a tender plant, and as a root out of dry ground: he hath no form nor comeliness; and when we shall see Him, there is no beauty that we should desire him.

"He is despised and rejected of men; a man of sorrows, and acquainted with grief: and we hid as it were our faces from him; he was despised, and we esteemed him not.

"Surely he hath borne our griefs, and carried our sorrows: yet we did esteem him stricken, smitten of God, and afflicted.

"But he was wounded for our transgressions, he was bruised for our iniquities: the chastisement of our peace was upon him; and with his stripes we are healed.

"All we like sheep have gone astray; we have turned every one to his own way; and the Lord hath laid on him the iniquity of us all.

"He was oppressed, and he was afflicted, yet he opened not his mouth: he is brought as a lamb to the slaughter, and as a sheep before her shearers is dumb, so he openeth not his mouth.

"He was taken from prison and from judgment: and who shall declare his generation? for he was cut off out of the land of the living: for the transgression[s] of my people was he stricken.

"And he made his grave with the wicked, and with the rich in his death; because he had done no violence, neither was any deceit in His mouth.

"Yet it pleased the Lord to bruise him; he hath put him to grief: when thou shalt make his soul an offering for sin, he shall see his seed, he shall prolong his days, and the pleasure of the Lord shall prosper in his hand.

"He shall see the travail of his soul, and shall be satisfied: by his knowledge shall my righteous servant justify many; for he shall bear their iniquities.

"Therefore will I divide Him a portion with the great, and he shall divide the spoil with the strong; because he hath poured out his soul unto death: and he was numbered with the transgressor[s]; and he bear the sin[s] of many, and made intercession for the transgressors."

I know that Jesus Christ lives and is our Savior. He has saved us. Though our sins may be as scarlet, indeed they can be as white as snow (Isaiah 1:18).

See Isaiah 53

Faith To Walk On Water

Have you ever felt your faith was just not enough to handle this stressful world? I have, and that's why this story gives me hope.

Jesus came walking on the Sea of Galilee, sometime around 3:00 in the morning. The disciples see Him, and, thinking He's a spirit, cry out in terror.

Jesus bids them, "Be of good cheer; it is I; be not afraid."

Peter, still wondering in the darkness if it was really the Master, asked if he might come out to the Savior on the water.

Jesus' answer was an invitation and a stretching. He said simply, "Come."

And Peter did it; he walked on the water, that is, as long as his gaze was fixed on the Master. But, the boisterous waves broke his concentration. In fear, he looked away from the Savior and immediately began to sink.

"Lord, save me!" He cried out.

The Lord stretched forth his hand, caught Peter, and lifted him back up on the water.

Together, they returned to the boat. Amazingly, the winds ceased and there followed a great calm.

Jesus said to Peter, "Oh thou of little faith, wherefore didst thou doubt?"

Some may think Peter failed. But did he, really? His effort increased his faith, and with the Master's gentle correction, he would succeed again.

And so it is with us. Our faith may falter for a time, and this stormy world might threaten to drown us; nonetheless, if we keep our eyes fixed resolutely on Him, and continue moving forward, He will not only save us, but will bring a great calm to our heart.

My faith may be small, but with Him, it's all I need.

See Matthew 14:25-31.

The Soil

Some time ago, in an effort to teach some high school students a difficult principle, I took them for a walk. As we strolled outside, I pointed out the beauties of the earth, the lush green grass, the tall majestic shade trees, and the delicate and beautiful flowers. To say that the students were less than impressed, would be an understatement. I think they suspected I was up to something.

When we were back in the classroom, I asked them what was responsible for all of the beauty and wonder outside. I got various answers. At that point, I walked over to one of my many potted plants in my classroom and took out a handful of soil. I asked them what it was.

I got the predictable answer, "dirt."

I explained to them that "dirt" is a dirty word to a soil scientist. "It's not dirt," I said. "It's soil."

I asked them to consider how important soil is to us. It didn't take very long to realize soil is a very precious commodity, responsible in large measure for life on this planet. Without it, most, if not all, of us wouldn't be here. It is the essence of life itself. Our bodies are made from the very dust of this earth. What do you owe to dirt? More than you think.

With their understanding of soil deepened, I took my soil, walked over to the nearest student and dumped it all over her desk, her books, and I think even her. Then, after scattering some of it around the room, the students looked at me a little shocked!

I gave them a moment to recover and asked, "All right, now what is it?"

Someone said something like this, "A mess."

I explained that soil, in its proper place and time, is a wonderful, God-given, life-sustaining, precious gift. But, when it's thrown in the middle of their living room, all over them, their family, and their carpet, it's just dirt; nothing more than cheap filth! It doesn't belong there.

So it is with human intimacy. Sexual relations between a man and a woman legally authorized by God are sacred, God-given, and precious. They are the wonderful source of life and unspeakable joy to God's children. But, when sex and the sacred are reduced to cheap entertainment, and callously thrown into my living room like so much digital dirt, no longer is it sacred. It is out of its place and time; it becomes filth. Any person who claims a right to pass on this evil has no right and has turned love into a lie.

For the sake of life on this planet, don't let them.

His Blood

From the moment this earth was formed, it was known man would make mistakes. It was no surprise all of us would break eternal laws and fall short of heavenly glory. Thus, a loving father sent His first-born son to this earth, with an endowment of power and a mission to save us all.

For centuries, the faithful brought their lambs to the holy place and killed them by shedding their life-blood. The knife in their hands and the blood upon the ground was a vivid reminder that someday, a damned and helpless humanity would shed the life-blood of the Son of God. His blood bought us, like money in a purchase. The ownership of our souls passed from the devil of hell to the deliverer of Heaven. We are His, bought with an infinite price. Is it any wonder we are continually reminded to remember His offering for us? But, oh how easy it is to neglect and to forget, especially when the image of blood and suffering is not before our eyes.

I was once trying to put a block of wood in my stove, when it slipped and smashed my thumb. The fingernail instantly turned purple and hurt—oh, it hurt! As the day wore on, the pain of my mistake intensified. Pressure built up under the nail, until the pain drove me to distraction. Finally, I took a knife and relieved the pressure. Off and on, for the next thirty-six hours, I tended to the wounded thumb.

Then came Sunday morning. I went to church and more or less forgot about the wounded thumb. The congregation began to sing a familiar hymn. My wife opened the book and handed it to me. I sang about half of the first verse. When I glanced down at the book, I was shocked to see the brilliant red of my blood on the stark white of the page. It was my thumb, again. Embarrassed, I quickly tried to clean it off.

Suddenly, I became aware of the words the congregation was sing-ing, "I tremble to know that for me He was crucified; that for me a sinner, He suffered; He bled and died." The hymn was "I Stand All Amazed." I stopped singing and looked at the blood on the page. The impression in my mind was too vivid for words.

I don't know what to make of this experience, but this much I know, the atonement of Christ really happened.

His blood was shed to save us from a fate worse than death. My blood on that page was only a few drops. By comparison, His blood was a torrent.

My blood was the result of my own foolishness. His blood heals the wounds of my foolishness.

My blood stained the page. His blood washes and cleanses all of our stains.

My blood and pain were only a moment. His blood and pain touched the infinite and the eternal.

By the grace of God, may we never forget the significance of His atoning blood.

The Cleansing

On the last Monday of the Lord's life, He entered the temple in Jerusalem and found in its courts a scene that angered Him. Flocks of cattle and sheep were milling and bawling; moneychangers, with their tables, exchanged current coinage for temple coinage so pilgrims might pay the temple tax. Haggling vendors hawked their wears in a scene that would remind us of carnivals at fair time. The noise, the stench, and especially the blasphemous desecration of holy ground moved the Lord to indignant anger. With whip and thunderous command, He drove them out into the streets where they belonged. No one dared oppose Him, not even the leaders of the Jews, whose pockets were being lined by the ill-gotten gain. Why? Because, in guilt there is weakness.

Twice the Lord cleansed the temple, once at the beginning of His ministry and again at the end. Is there a broader parallel? The Lord "cleaned house" once on this earth with a flood. The second time it will be with fire—and clean it will be. Of that we may be assured.

The second story takes place the following day, Tuesday. While in the precincts of the temple, He prophesies the total destruction of the temple and denounces the leaders of the Jews for their hypocrisy and corruption. Upon leaving the temple, He retires to the solitude of the Mount of Olives. As He sat, probably looking over the city, His disciples come to Him privately and ask Him when the temple would be destroyed. When would the prophecy be fulfilled? What would be the signs of His second coming? The Savior's answers to those questions constitute Matthew 24 and what we call the discourse on "the signs of the times."

It is worthwhile to look carefully at the emotional aftermath His answer had on the disciples. He describes to the twelve such horrible things as "wars and rumors of wars," and "the whole earth in commotion," and "men's hearts failing them for fear just before His coming." He speaks of "the love of men" in our day "waxing cold," and "iniquity abounding," of "earthquakes and desolating sicknesses," and "men killing one another." When He finishes, the apostles are visibly scared and upset. Jesus calms them by saying, "Be not troubled, for, when all these things come to pass, you may know that the promises which have been made unto you shall be fulfilled" (D&C 45:35).

If the original twelve apostles were troubled by those signs of the times, most of which would not even occur in their lifetime, how much more understandable it is that we, in whose day they are being fulfilled, should be troubled. Yet, there is no need to let either the signs or the flood of wickedness and corruption around us unduly concern us. Be assured, the Good Shepherd is right on schedule, and He has not abandoned the flock just because of a little bad weather and some ravening wolves among us. Remember, He said, "Be not troubled" (Matthew 24:6).

Tooth Fairy

We have been commanded by our Father in Heaven to "ask, and ye shall receive" (John 16:24), to make all our wants and wishes known to Him. Still, there is a need for judgment and wisdom in how we pray and what we pray for.

Not long ago, I was traveling back from Wyoming, when my cell phone rang. I answered. It was my wife wondering where I was. As we talked, I could hear one of my younger children in the background.

"I wanna talk to Daddy. I wanna talk to Daddy."

Finally my wife said, "Shaina wants to talk to you."

"Guess what, Daddy," she said when she came on the phone.

"What?"

"I lost a tooth."

"You did!"

"Yup."

"You mean you got a hole in your face now?"

"Yup."

I said to her, "So, how much do you want the tooth fairy to give you for that tooth?"

She thought for a second, and then very matter-of-factly she announced, "Fifty dollars!"

"Fifty dollars!" I said, a little shocked.

"Yup," she said flatly, as if to say, "I've made up my mind, Dad, and this is not negotiable."

After losing her tooth earlier that afternoon at the fair, Shaina had explained to her mother the following, "Mommy, I'm all grown up now. I'm going to kindergarten, I can ride a two-wheeler, and I lost a tooth. I'm big now!"

Sometimes I wonder if we get a little big for our britches with our Father in Heaven, maybe just a little thoughtless in our prayers. I wonder if, at times, we don't take the time to think very carefully about what we're saying, or sometimes we act as though God works on the same premise as the tooth fairy or Santa Claus.

The most perfect kind of prayer is inspired prayer. It is the kind of prayer borne of sincere effort, which brings our mind and heart into union with our Father in Heaven, and brings us to ask for nothing more than what He already wants to give us.

South Teton

When the Savior said, "Be ye therefore perfect" (Matthew 5:48), some of us may have misunderstood, and it is costing us dearly.

For a long time, I have wanted to stand atop each of those famous peaks in western Wyoming, the Tetons. A couple of years ago, I was privileged to climb the tallest, the Grand, and I don't hesitate to say, it was a life-changing experience.

I had a young friend who not only knew the route to the summit of the other peaks, but was also willing to take me along. I had the desire, the strength, and the will to climb all along, but I knew better than to go wandering around up there without a guide.

On the appointed day, we set out for the top. By day's end, we would have ascended 6500 vertical feet and traveled somewhere between ten and twenty miles.

As we climbed, our guide, Luke, pointed out the trail and moved up and down the line, encouraging and helping each of the members of our party. He insisted periodically that we stop, rest, and drink plenty of water. There was wisdom in this, even though we didn't feel like resting. During those times, we were not only able to rest, but we were also able to look back at how far we had climbed and marvel at the view below us. It gave us a chance to laugh, to joke, and to talk with each other. Little did we know, but these were vital times of refreshing. How vital, we would not know until later.

By noon, we reached the Garnet Canyon saddle between the middle and south peaks. After a quick lunch, we set out on the last leg of the climb and, I might add, the steepest. Dark clouds threatened bad weather, making it necessary that we waste absolutely no time. I watched some in our climbing party push themselves way too hard, and altitude sickness began to overcome them. Headaches, nausea, and fatigue nearly brought them to their knees. Prudently, the whole group slowed and balanced our pace at the optimum, pushing as hard as we could, but resting sufficiently so we could still keep everyone in the party climbing.

Our efforts were rewarded. At 2:00 that afternoon, we summited the South Teton, happy as can be, satisfied at our accomplishment, and more than a little awed at the grandeur that lay before our eyes.

Earlier in the day, it was hard to listen to the guide at the bottom when he said "Rest and drink." We felt good. We didn't need to stop; we could push on; we were men! Nevertheless, we did obey, and that careful conservation of energy eventually brought all of us to stand on top. It made no difference to me who got there first, as long as we all got there, and we did!

Perfection is the highest mountain in our eternity. We'll be there. It not only cannot be climbed without the constant guidance of one who has climbed it before, the Savior, but it is also infinitely more than a one day or a one lifetime jaunt. I believe, as I was once told, that, "given enough time and enough people who love you, perfection is not only probable, it is inevitable" (L. Edward Brown).

However, if there is no joy in the journey now, maybe you're pushing it too hard!

The Easter Story

It's Easter, and our opportunity to tell the greatest story of hope ever told.

In spite of the midday hour, darkness covers the land of Jerusalem and many of the hearts of the people. The Lord Jesus hangs in incomprehensible agony on the cross of Calvary. Standing near the cross is his mother and Mary Magdalene, those devoted and beloved women who accompanied Him. Their sufferings are surely grievous as they helplessly watch Him die. During those awful three hours from noon to 3:00 p.m., on that Friday afternoon, Jesus is again afflicted with the exacting pain of the atonement for the sins of mankind. It is horrible! And then, somewhere around 3:00 p.m., He cries out with a loud voice, "My God, my God, why hast thou forsaken me" (Matthew 27:46)?

The Father has withdrawn, leaving the victory entirely to the Son. The Lord Jesus has now descended to the very depths, the lowest He can go.

Shortly after that, The Savior, knowing that all things were now accomplished, declared, "Father, it is finished, thy will is done" (JST Matthew 27:50), "into thy hands I commend my spirit" (Luke 23:46). The Savior gave up the Ghost, His spirit passing at that moment into the spirit paradise He had so recently spoken of to the penitent thief.

It is now late Friday afternoon. Quickly, His disciples and friends take His body down from the cross and hastily place it in a borrowed tomb. The Saturday Sabbath begins shortly. For the few remaining hours of Friday, all of Saturday, and until sometime in the predawn hours of Sunday, or in other words, over three days time, the Master's body lies in the tomb while His disciples hide and grieve.

Then, the miracle of all miracles, Jesus returns and takes up that broken and destroyed body, bringing it forth in resurrected perfection and glory. Though it certainly was not necessary to release Him from the tomb, the angels come and roll back the stone that sealed the tomb.

It is now just before dawn. Mary Magdalene and the other women come down to the garden tomb, bringing spices to finish the preparation of His body for proper burial. They walked along, wondering as they go, who will roll back the huge stone to give them entrance? As they approach the tomb in the dim light, not only is the stone already rolled back, but two men, whose countenances were as brilliant as lightning, are sitting on the stone. The angels say to them, "He is not here: for he is risen...Come, see the place where the Lord lay" (Matthew 28:6). The angels continue, "Go quickly, and tell his disciples that he is risen from the dead" (Matthew 28:7).

Mary leaves the tomb, evidently not completely understanding what it means. She runs and tells Peter and John, "They have taken away the Lord out of the sepulcher, and we know not where they have laid him" (John 20:2). Jesus had told them repeatedly He would rise again the third day. But they don't understand; how could they? Such a thing has never occurred in the history of mankind.

Peter and John leave immediately and run to the tomb, and sure enough, the tomb is empty. They return home, leaving Mary there alone at the tomb. Mary stoops down, weeping out of grief and loss, and peers into the darkened tomb. The linen grave clothes lie as they were, the body of Christ having passed through them.

The two angels, evidently not visible to Peter and John, are sitting where the body of Jesus had lain. They speak to her, "Woman, why weepest thou? She sayeth unto them, Because they have taken away [the body of] my Lord, and I know not where they have laid him" (John 20:13).

At that moment, Mary perceives someone behind her. She turns around. It is, she supposes at a glance, the gardener. He speaks to her, "Woman, why weepest thou? Whom seekest thou?" (John 20:15).

Mary supposes again that this is the gardener and says to Him, "Sir, if thou hast borne him hence, tell me where thou hast laid him, and I will take him away" (John 20:15).

It's Jesus, but she doesn't know that. And then, He says only one word to her, but oh, the significance and the familiarity of that word. He says simply, "Mary" (John 20:16).

Instantly, she recognizes Him, and her tears of pain and loss are transformed into those of the most transcendent joy. She runs to Him.

"Rabboni," she cries out, meaning, "My beloved Master" (John 20:16). And indeed, He was to her, and indeed He must be to us.

Mary's world changed forever at that moment, as did ours. Can you imagine the significance of her seeing Him? Everything He had ever taught—everything now had greater authority, greater power, greater believability. He was no longer dead. He was a living person of flesh and bone. And because He was, so will we. All our eternal possibilities stand or fall on the reality and the truth of His resurrection. This is the core center of Christianity.

I declare to you, "He lives, and while He lives I'll sing." Joy, power, peace, priesthood, and love and family do not end with the grave, because of Him. "He lives all glory to His name; He lives, my Savior still the same. Oh, sweet the joy this sentence gives: I Know That My Redeemer Lives" (LDS Hymn #136).

Adapted from Matthew, Mark, Luke, & John.

Prodigal Son

Personal discipleship requires difficult changes throughout life. More difficult is the change necessary for one who's been trapped by a lifestyle. Such is the parable of the Prodigal Son.

As the rebellious son came to himself and realized his folly, he determined to go home and beg forgiveness and employment of his father. At least, he might eat decently. He set out for home.

The scripture records that while "he was yet a great way off, his father saw him, and had compassion, and ran" and threw himself upon the boy's neck. The father kissed him, heard his confessions, and rejoicing, brought him once more into the family circle.

How did that father even know he was coming, unless he'd been watching for him? Anxiously, the father had watched and waited, and the moment the boy came into view, the father ran all the way out to meet him, quick to forgive.

So it is with our Heavenly Father. He is not sternly aloof, withholding His love until the very last steps of repentance are walked. He doesn't demand of us to take every return step alone. He loves us so compellingly that our first feeble steps in His direction are answered with marathons in return. No one returns to the fold alone.

If, when through repentance people return, our celebrations could be as festive and forgiving as those in Heaven, maybe more people would undertake the journey.

See Luke 15:11-32

But If Not

There are three words from the Old Testament that have a uniquely deep significance. They are the words "but if not."

In the ancient province of Babylon, King Nebuchadnezzar set up a ninety foot golden image and commanded all the people of his kingdom, including the Hebrews, to worship the statue at the sound of certain music. If they did not, they would die in the fiery furnaces that same hour by the king's decree.

The statue was unveiled in all its splendor, and at the given signal, the people bowed before the idol. Everyone, that is, except three faithful Hebrews, Shadrach, Meshach, and Abed-nego. They refused to bow, and of course, were accused before the king. They were brought before him, and the king offered them a chance to comply and bow before the idol. He threatened them again with the fiery furnace if they did not.

There was no hesitation in their reply. They said, "Nebuchadnezzar...our God whom we serve is able to deliver us from the burning fiery furnace, and He will deliver us out of thine hand, O King. But if not, be it known unto thee, O King, that we will not serve thy gods, nor worship the golden image which thou hast set up" (Daniel 3:16-18).

It was not the answer the king wanted to hear. In a rage, he commanded the furnace be heated seven times hotter than usual and had them cast in. So hot was the furnace, it killed the soldiers who threw them in, but Shadrach, Meshach, and Abed-nego fell into the furnace and were unharmed. They were delivered by the angel of God.

In the example of these three men, there's a lesson in faith that can be understood. They said to the king in essence, "We know God has the power to deliver us, but whether His will is that we live or die, we don't know. But, it makes no difference. No matter how hot the furnace, we will still trust Him and not yield to wickedness. Burn us if you will!"

God bless those mighty heroes among us now, those who submit sweetly to God's will, praying and hoping for miracles of deliverance from life's fiery trials. But, if they're not forthcoming, they are still true!

Gideon

For those of you working hard on New Year's resolutions or just trying to improve yourself, a key to success is found in the story of Gideon, the mighty warrior of Israel's past.

A people called the Midianites had conquered Israel and destroyed their land, leaving them with little food. The Lord came to a young man, a farm-boy named Gideon, and called him to free Israel. Gideon humbly protested the Lord's choice, not feeling worthy, but the Lord made it known to him that he was indeed the man chosen to free Israel.

Gideon subsequently gathered an army of 32,000 men to go to war against the Midianites and drive them out of the land. The Midianites, however, came into the land with an army of 135,000 men.

Strangely, the Lord spoke to Gideon and told him he had too many men. Too many men! The odds were four to one against Gideon, and the Lord says he has too many men!

Obediently, Gideon steps forward and asks his assembled troops how many of them are afraid to go into battle. Twenty-two thousand men raise their hands, and Gideon sends them home. He is now left with an army of 10,000 against an army of 135,000. That makes the odds approximately thirteen to one.

Still, the Lord says to Gideon, "The people are yet too many" (Judges 7:4).

He then reduces Gideon's army to a measly three hundred men. The odds are now four hundred fifty to one.

The Lord says to Gideon, "By the three hundred...will I save you, and deliver the Midianites into thine hand" (Judges 7:7).

Why? The Lord does not waste words or time or effort. There had to be a reason for this. Why does He do this to Gideon? The story continues.

Gideon takes his three hundred men and divides them into three companies, giving each man a lantern, a trumpet, and a pitcher used for holding water. Late that night, after the Midianites have gone to bed, Gideon's men come down off the mountain and surround the Midianite camp.

Suddenly, at Gideon's signal, each man breaks his pitcher, waves his lantern, blows his trumpet, and shouts, "The sword of the Lord, and of Gideon" (Judges 7:20).

Can you imagine the chaos that exploded in the Midianite camp? They bailed out of bed in stark terror, grabbing their swords as they ran. While Gideon and his men make all the noise and commotion they can, the Midianites, in the darkness and confusion, can't tell friend from foe and start running around killing each other.

When it's all over, 135,000 Midianites are driven and dead, and Israel is free. So grateful are the Lord's people they offer to make Gideon and his sons kings. Although he declines, he does lead Israel in peace and righteousness for the next forty years. Gideon became a legend in Israel.

Why did the Lord reduce Gideon's number? Because it had to be with Gideon as it must be with us. We must know, as Gideon had to know, our victories in the large and small battles of life are fought and won by the Lord, not us!

You cannot win alone! Whether it be the small battle of a habit, or the major war against the natural man, victory will come to those warriors, and only to those warriors, who rely on the Lord of Hosts, the God of battles.

See Judges 6-8.

Band-aids And Sunsets

One autumn morning, I stood transfixed and watched the first glorious rays of the sun break the horizon. Oh, it was beautiful! I felt a surge of joy. It was invigorating. That night, at 6:56 p.m., from a commanding overlook, I watched that same blazing sun sink below the horizon. It was a strange mix of feelings. As its last rays disappeared, I felt a strange sense of loss, almost a feeling of panic, especially as I turned and looked over the city below me. The brilliant colors that were there a moment ago were gone. The whole city was bathed in darkness and gloom.

Ours is a world of stark contrasts. The earth, in its natural state, is a thing of beauty; it was created by God. It bears glorious witness of its Creator. Yet, for all of its beauty, the sun is setting on the society that inhabits it. Our civilization plunges deeper and deeper into darkness, gloom, and filth. What do we do? What can we do?

Not long ago, I overheard a conversation between members of my family and a friend. They were complaining about the ills and evils of certain television programs. I stood and listened. After some time, they dispersed, and I walked into the room.

One of my daughters looked at me, and she said, "Dad, my stomach hurts."

At that moment, a bizarre idea struck me. Dad is always a teacher.

"I know just what to do," I said, and I ran upstairs.

When I returned, I asked her to show me exactly where it hurt. As she did, I pulled a Band-Aid out of my pocket, and I stuck it on her tummy. She gave me the strangest look.

"There," I said with triumph, "doesn't that feel better?"

"No," she said laughing.

"It doesn't?" I said, playing stupid. "Well, then I know just what'll fix it for sure."

She laughed even harder when I bent over and kissed her tummy "boo-boo."

I looked up at her to see if she understood what I was doing. Not surprisingly, she was completely clueless. She had no idea what I was doing. So I reminded her of the recent gripe session about the television program.

It took a few minutes, but she came to see that griping and whining about the world's problems are just about as effective as a Band-Aid on a bellyache.

"Don't gripe!" I said. "Do something!"

There are too many in this world today who just want to kiss society's boo-boos and hope they'll go away. They won't! Hasn't history taught us anything?

Those with the power of truth must be doctors to a sick and dying world or be responsible for the death of it. Come, all ye sons and daughters of God who bear the covenant of Abraham. The sun is nigh to setting.

Courage To Do Right

Some time ago, one of my daughters ran into a difficult situation with some friends who wanted to watch a movie with a questionable rating. When asked her opinion, she said she didn't want to watch it. It turned out she was the only one who didn't, and you can probably guess what happened next. The others began to pressure her, saying things like, "You haven't even seen it. How can you judge it?" Some of them even got mad at her.

Feeling badly, she wondered if she had done the right thing. Should she have spoken up or simply kept quiet for the sake of peace?

A few days after she told me what happened, I was reading in the scriptures. A story about the Savior jumped out at me and took on a whole new meaning.

One Sabbath Day, Jesus went into the synagogue to teach, and, as always, some of His enemies were there. Sitting in the meeting was a man who had a crippled hand. The Savior's enemies watched Him carefully, just to see if He would heal the man on the Sabbath Day, which they considered a very great sin.

The Savior knew what they were thinking. He knew if He healed the man they'd be offended, and there would be trouble.

Jesus could have ignored the man with the withered hand. He didn't have to help him. He didn't have to say anything. No one would have thought any less of Him if He had simply finished His teaching and gone on His way. After all, He didn't heal every afflicted person He encountered.

But, the Savior had more courage than that. He had the courage to do the right thing, even if it would make others mad. He said to the man with the withered hand, "Stand forth."

The man stood up. Jesus then faced His enemies and asked them if it was wrong to do good. He stood there looking at them as He waited for their response. They refused to answer. What could they say?

Jesus turned to the afflicted man and said, "Stretch forth thine hand."

As the man stretched out his hand, it was instantly healed and made whole.

The Savior's enemies were so mad they got up and stomped out of the meeting. Their anger would have been bad enough, but they also began putting together a plan to kill Him. The Savior had to leave the area just to stay alive.

Doing the right thing to show off is self-righteous, and that is very wrong. However, doing right, when you could get away with doing wrong, even if it does offend people, that's what it means to be righteous, and that will always take great courage.

See Mark 3:1-7.

Love One Another

On the very night Jesus would be delivered up to cruel men to be spit upon, beaten, whipped, tortured, and finally killed, the Savior made this crowning pronouncement to His disciples. Knowing full well His fate, He said, "By this shall all men know that ye are my disciples, if ye have love one to another" (John 13:35).

He called it a "new commandment," and it was. Love was to be re-enthroned once more among the Jews to its rightful place, not as a gospel garnishment, but as an essential driving, vital force in the Kingdom of God. The love the Master intended was to be much more than something we said, much more than an affectionate feeling, it was to be the kind of love this simple story illustrates.

Grandpa had a date with his four-year-old grandson. They were going to go out for the evening, just the two of them, to a local Salt Lake dance festival.

All was well for a time, but after two hours, the little boy got tired of just sitting there. All that music and dancing just wasn't very interesting to him. He began to squirm and to wiggle, and he wanted to wander off. Well, Grandpa didn't want that, so he tried to hold on to the little guy. This only made him more difficult. The little guy began to scream and holler.

Suddenly, without any warning, the toddler doubled up his fist and smacked his grandfather right in the side of the head.

"Grandfather," he shouted, "don't shove me!"

Well, that really rang Grandpa's chimes and woke him right up. His first impulse, he said, was "that the little rascal ought to be spanked."

Then he remembered something he had seen the little boy's mother do. Rather than give the little guy what some would deem he deserved, Grandpa reached out and gathered him into a tender embrace and loved him. In only a moment, the little boy quieted and softened. His chubby little arms reached up and went around Grandpa's neck in complete surrender.

How difficult is such a response? It is exactly as hard to do as it is effective. Returning meanness for meanness only yields more meanness. The world was changed once by love, one soul at a time. Why can't it be done again?

As Grandpa Harold B. Lee said it, "If you want to save, that's the method."

See The Teachings of Harold B. Lee, edited by Clyde J. Williams, Salt Lake City, Utah: Bookcraft, 1996.

Summer Thunder

Last summer, while in Salt Lake City for some meetings, my wife and I decided to go to Temple Square to look around. As we drove, I noticed off to the west a big thunderstorm coming in. We arrived just before it hit.

I love thunderstorms. I love to watch them, especially the lightning. When I got there, I wanted to watch the lightning, but I didn't want to get soaked in the process. Then I got an idea. I ran all the way across Temple Square to the north visitors' center and up to the second floor rotunda, the one that has all the windows. I got there just as the storm hit, and it was a storm! The trees whipped violently in the wind. The rain came down in sheets. It was genuinely funny watching people running for cover. But, the most captivating thing of all was the lightning. It wasn't intermittent. It was almost continuous, and it was close! It even knocked out the power to part of the city. I became thoroughly engrossed in the storm.

Suddenly, I was startled by a voice from behind me and above me. It said, "Learn of me; listen to my words; walk in the meekness of my spirit, and you shall have peace in me."

The timing and effect of those words coming over the sound system was powerful. I became cognoscente of where I was. I turned around and found myself standing directly in front of the statue of the Christus. It was a very unique situation.

Outside, beyond those windows, it was dark, violent, a frightening world. Inside where I was, I felt only safety, peace, and calmness. I had no fear of the lightning. I stepped closer to the statue, right between His outstretched arms and looked up into His face. For some reason, my eyes were drawn to the prints of the nails in His hands and His feet and the spear mark in His side.

I can't tell you what I felt. I don't know how. But I can tell you this, I am convinced there is nothing I will ever be able to do to even remotely repay or deserve what He has so freely given. I may be stuck, for now, in a thunderstorm world, but I don't have to live running around scared. If I come to the Savior, I will always find peace and security in His shelter, and joy in the arms of His love.

Naaman's Miracle

Naaman was not a Jew. Naaman was a gentile. He was not a worshipper of Jehovah either. He was a pagan idol-worshipper. As a leader of Syria's army, Naaman had delivered his nation out of the hands of the Assyrians. He was considered a great and a good man.

However, Naaman was a leper. In that day and time, leprosy was called the living death. There was no known cure, that is, until one day, when a little Israelite girl in Naaman's house, who served Naaman's wife, made the following comment, "Would God my Lord were with the prophet that is in Samaria! For he would recover him of his leprosy" (2 Kings 5:3).

Naaman heard about what the servant girl said. With a glimmering shred of a last hope and a small fortune, Naaman sets out for Israel, the prophet, and a cure. Riding in the horse drawn chariot, symbolizing his power and position, Naaman comes to the door of Elisha's house. From within, the prophet sends a messenger, telling him to dip himself seven times in the Jordan River.

Indignant and outraged the prophet wouldn't even so much as come out to meet him, Naaman turns away and starts for home in a huff. Well, it just so happened that the way home took him relatively near the Jordan River.

As he passes near the Jordan, one of Naaman's servants approaches him and says with respect, "My father, if the prophet had bid thee do some great thing, wouldest thou not have done it? How much rather then, when he saith to thee, Wash and be clean" (2 Kings 5:13)?

This was an eternally critical moment for Naaman. Had he shrugged off the counsel of his servant and ignored the prophet, there would likely have been no miracle on Naaman's behalf. No one would know of the man today. Yet, Naaman made a decision.

He steps into the water and lowers not only his body, but his haughty pride as well. Seven times he dips his body into that filthy water. Then, as he rises the seventh time, the scripture records, "He was clean." The leprosy was gone.

Now, as then, the Lord's messengers ask us to do some things that make us look pretty silly in the eyes of the world, all the while extending marvelous promises to us and to our families if we will be obedient.

Did Naaman's leprosy vanish on the first washing? The second? The third? The sixth? No. It was the seventh time.

Our greatest test in this life is probably not going to be the great challenge that comes once. But rather, our greatest test in this life is probably going to be the little side journeys of time and obedience, like going to Church, reading the scriptures daily and praying daily, those things which may seem inconsequential. Yet, eventually they will add up to seven, and a miracle!

See 2 Kings 5

Jed's Prayer

The Lord says in the scriptures, "ask, and ye shall receive" (John 16:24). I suppose most of us have figured out how to ask, but I wonder how many of us have figured out how to recognize the answer. Our Father can answer His children any way He chooses, but it would be well to learn how He most frequently answers us.

Not long ago, my wife was helping a friend with a project at the church. They found they had need of a hot glue-gun, which my wife had at home. Not having her car, Debbie borrowed Mindy's car and took off for home.

As she pulled up in front of the house, she left the car running, thinking since she knew exactly where the glue-gun was, she would only be a moment. So with the car running, she closed the door and ran in the house, not realizing as she did so, the car's doors automatically locked.

When she came back out, of course, she couldn't get in. She looked at the coded keypad on the door and thought there was no way she'd be able to guess the right numbers, so she didn't even try. She went back in and tried to reach Mindy by phone, but no one answered.

In desperation, she turned to Jed, our teenage son, and asked him to get on his bike, ride up to the church, and get the door's number code.

Jed stepped outside. It was 2:30 in the afternoon, and it was hot! There was no way Jed wanted to pedal two miles just for some numbers.

Interestingly enough, Jed offered a prayer to Heavenly Father asking Him for help. No sooner had the "amen" been said, when a series of numbers came into Jed's mind. He stepped up to the door, punched in those numbers on the five-button, ten-digit keypad and tried the door.

What do you think happened?

The door opened!

If we expect the blatant and spectacular to answer our prayers, we likely will not be attuned to the quiet little voice that stirs thoughts in our minds and feelings in our hearts. So subtle are these thoughts, we often pass them by, thinking they come from us, from within our own minds, and not from God. If we will learn to look inward, and listen to the thoughts in our minds, and the feelings in our hearts, a whole new world will open up. It's called the "spirit of revelation."

Cattle Drive

I remember, as a boy growing up on a ranch in southeastern Idaho, going on cattle drives with my dad. Every year we had this ritual where we drove them to and from the summer pastures. It was an exciting time for me, so much so that I never minded always being the one appointed to bring up the rear and eat the dust. I remember one drive in particular where we didn't reach the home pastures until shortly after dark. Tired and ready for a rest, I headed for the barn. However, my dad asked me to stay behind and watch the herd.

I protested; I wanted to go home. "Why?" I said. "There's fences. They're not going anywhere."

He explained the cows and their calves had become separated during the drive. By instinct, he said, they would return to the last place they had seen each other in an effort to "mother-up" as he called it. It would be necessary for me to stay behind, ride the fence, and keep them in the pasture until all the cows found their calves. Well, I didn't think it'd be that big of a deal, and it was dark anyway. Surely they would bed right down.

I was wrong, very wrong! I remember clearly to this day running my horse blindly back and forth in the dark, along that fence, trying to keep those cows and calves in. So deter-  mined were they that they would stick their heads in the smallest hole and plow right on through. It was a scary, grueling night, and years later it became a powerful learning experience. The familial bond between those cows and calves was so strong they would fight their way through any obstacle to find each other. The noise of an entire herd, cows and calves calling to each other, was deafening.

Over the years, I've thought a lot about that experience. I don't think it's a whole lot different with people. We are the children of God. He is our Father, literally. Contrary to what is taught, we are not accidents of nature—some sort of half-breed chimpanzee. God is part of us, and we of Him. He has planted within each of us a homing instinct, a drive if you will, that yearns for Him and our Heavenly home, for the peace, happiness, and love we once enjoyed in His presence. He is calling us. Those who will honestly listen, will hear Him. If we doggedly persist each day in calling to Him, and breaching every fence that gets in our way, there will come a day, a day of joy, when He will welcome us home with open arms.

Storms Of Life

James, the Lord's brother, once said, "Count it all joy when ye fall into many afflictions" (JST James 1:2). Joy? Where is the joy in life's storms? What eternal purpose is served by fear, pain, and struggle?

Years ago, a young friend of mine, a former student, was climbing in the Teton mountain range. She and her sisters weren't far from the top of Table Mountain when they noticed a thunderstorm, big and black, coming up behind them.

Those who are familiar with the Tetons know lightning storms are deadly. Stories and legends of killer storms are familiar to anyone who has spent much time there.

As the storm bore down on them, my friend Skye became anxious and frightened. Should she and her sisters go on to the top and take their chances with the lightning, or should they turn back and get down to lower, safer ground?

They had come all this way; they were so close to the summit, but the summit would be most dangerous in such a storm. This was more than just a fear of getting wet. People have died in those mountains from such storms.

Why did the storm have to come in the first place? Couldn't an all-powerful, all-knowing God have turned it away? He knew it was there. Couldn't He have turned it away? Of course He could. So why didn't He? Moreover, why does He allow Satan to oppose everything we are and everything we do? In other words, why does life have to be so hard sometimes? The answer may be found in another story.

A man was once brought to Jesus who was deaf and had a speech impediment. Jesus took the man aside from the group and put His fingers into the man's ears. He then spit and touched the saliva to the man's tongue. Then the Savior sighed, looked up to Heaven, and said, "Be opened" (Mark 7:34). The man was immediately healed.

Why did He put the fingers in the man's ears, and why did He put the spit on the man's tongue? The man was deaf. In a sense, his ears were plugged. By putting His fingers in the man's ears, Jesus communicated His intent to remove the obstruction so the man could hear. It was a form of communication. Why did He put the saliva on the tongue? Then and now saliva symbolizes healing. Touching saliva to the man's tongue communicated the message that Jesus wanted to heal his speech impediment.

Why did Jesus do these unusual and, some would say, disgusting things? The answer is this: If there is no faith, Jesus can do no miracle. Within that man, the sleeping giant of faith had to be awakened before the miracle could happen. It's the same now. God will do whatever it takes to awaken faith in us, even if that means trials, afflictions, fear, and even thunderstorms when we least expect or want them.

As the storm closed in on the girls, Skye and her sisters huddled together, got down on their knees and prayed and asked their Father in Heaven to turn the storm away. Their awakened faith was answered as they stood and watched the mighty storm divide and go around them on all sides. Rain fell and lightning flashed around them, but where they stood it was dry and safe. They continued on to the top, and later, from the summit of Table Mountain, they watched the storm come back together in all of its fury and lash the peaks of the three Tetons.

That storm became one of the most spiritual experiences in my young friend's life. So it can be with us. Don't curse the storms in life, whatever they are and however they come. Use them. Turn to God in faith and prayer, the God whose love never fails, and let Him awaken the sleeping, divine giant within you.

See Mark 7:32-37.

The Power Of His Name

A name is an interesting thing; it's more than just a word. A name is a symbol of the person who bears it. The more acquainted I become with you, the more the seeing or hearing of your name will affect me. Now with that in mind, there is one name we frequently hear and speak as Christians more important than any other on earth. Please consider the following example.

After the Savior's resurrection and ascension into heaven, Peter and John were one day entering the temple. It was around 3:00 in the afternoon. As they passed through the gate called "beautiful," they saw a man lame from his birth, begging for a handout.

Peter stopped and said to the man, "Look on us."

The man looked at them expecting to receive something; and most likely did not expect what he got.

Peter then said, "Silver and gold have I none; but such as I have give I thee: In the name of Jesus Christ of Nazareth rise up and walk."

Peter took the man by the hand "and lifted him up" and immediately his legs received strength, and he stood for the first time in his life. Peter performed no corrective surgery, nor did he apply any kind of a brace to help the man stand. He simply spoke a name in faith, and a power was unleashed and set in motion that flowed into the body of the man and healed him. Obviously, it was no ordinary name.

When word got out of what Peter had done, he was questioned by the Jews.

"By what power, or by what name, have ye done this?" They asked.

Boldly, Peter declared, "By the name of Jesus Christ of Nazareth... doth this man stand here before you whole." Peter then added this vital truth, "there is none other name under heaven given among men, whereby we must be saved."

I wonder sometimes if we use that name as though it were nothing more than a way to end a talk or close a prayer. I hope not. I hope we understand His sacred name represents and unlocks the power and authority of God unto our happiness and salvation. All the power of the atonement is embodied within that name. No wonder we are commanded to be careful how we use it.

See Acts 3-4.

I Love You

Do these words sound familiar? "Come unto me all ye that labor and are heavy laden, and I will give you rest" (Matthew 11:28). Those words are true.

Not long ago, someone I know had a simple, yet profound experience. Like many of you, he has many responsibilities that vary from urgencies to emergencies, depending on the day. It's all he can do most times just to keep up, let alone get it all done well.

On this particular day, he had begun the morning sometime around 5:30 a.m., and had run frantically all day long with the responsibilities of the day. That night, as he knelt in a private place to pray, he poured out his heart to his Father in Heaven, expressing thanks and seeking strength. The prayer was not unusual. It was typical of so many thousands he had offered before. However, as he closed the prayer in the name of the Savior and said "amen," in the split second before he could rise to his feet, a voice as clear and distinct as mine came into his mind.

It said simply, "I love you."

The most compelling feeling of love accompanied the voice. Not only did he hear the words in his mind, but a feeling of love, warmth, and comfort, something like a heavenly hug, filled his soul. Tears came to eyes that seldom cry. For a few minutes, he remained on his knees basking in the heavenly embrace, letting it wash over and through him. When he finally arose, the burden was gone. His entire outlook was changed. Peace, happiness, and confidence replaced the exhausted despair that had been there only a few minutes before. He could do it. Once again, he could go on and face another day. The burden no longer seemed so heavy.

God is there, and He hears us and He answers our prayers. He loves us. It is not only possible, but inevitable that He will help us carry our burdens, even the mundane ones, if we will work as if all depends on us, and pray as if it all depends on Him.

The Skunk

Many years ago, when I was just a boy growing up on the ranch, a friend and I came upon a skunk caught in a trap. The little critter was so hopelessly tangled in the fence he couldn't move an inch, at least so I thought. I decided I was going to let that skunk go. I had done this before, and I knew if I was careful, I could do it again. Care-

fully and ever so slowly, I crept toward the skunk. His angry beady little eyes never left me. I got down within inches of him and knelt down to release him.

My fingers were just clos-ing around the trap, when my friend spoke loudly and abruptly from behind me. "Hey, you're never going to get him out of there!"

To say the least, he startled me. But what's worse, he startled the skunk! The little beast whirled and sprayed me, hitting me squarely in the face and the chest. I fell back spitting, gagging, and choking! Yuck! I still remember that taste!

Well, from there, the rest is kind of a blur. I remember heading for home as fast as I could go, stripping off my coat and my clothes all the way across the lawn and into the house. I ran straight for the shower. I scrubbed and scrubbed until the hot water ran out, and then I scrubbed some more. I came out of the shower as rosy and pink as the sunburst nose of a child, and you know, I thought I'd done it. When I got through, I couldn't smell a thing.

One day not long after that, I was at school playing some basketball with friends. We were playing hard and sweating pretty heavily.

Suddenly, one of my friends said something like this, "Oo, you smell that? It smells like a skunk!"

Everyone looked around, but there was no skunk in the room, that is, except this redheaded one. His spray was in my hair, and for months after, whenever I got hot and sweaty, I smelled like a skunk.

That experience taught me one of the most fundamental lessons of mortal life. When you keep company with skunks, you stink!

What are you keeping company with? Are you surrounding yourself with influences that stink? The music we listen to, the books we read, and the stuff we bring into our world will either make us happy, or they will leave us with the depressing stench of a fallen world. Remember, you can no more be happy surrounded by filth than you can smell like roses when playing with skunks!

See Mark 5:1-20

Power

The most awesome displays of man's power shrink in comparison to the power of God.

During the Savior's ministry, He was once accosted by a man possessed by a legion of devils. The afflicted man was widely known in the area as a crazy and wild man. He lived naked in the mountains and tombs, continually crying and cutting himself with stones. Any previous attempts to restrain and tame him had been answered with super-human strength. As he broke the chains and escaped, he was more of an animal than a man.

However, in the presence of the Savior, the possessed man fell at His feet and worshipped Him.

At the Master's rebuke, the many devils possessing the man's body requested permission to enter the bodies of a herd of pigs feeding on the mountains nearby. The Savior granted it, whereupon the swine ran off the cliff into the sea and drowned themselves.

When the townspeople come out to investigate, they discover the wild man sitting, clothed, and in his right mind. They are shocked and afraid at the dramatic events and send Jesus away without hearing a word.

As to the man, he asked to accompany the Savior, but was instead sent back to his family, rejoicing. The Master and His disciples then departed. It appears that the Master's sole purpose that day in crossing the Sea of Galilee was to rescue one soul beyond mortal help.

By the power of His word, He cleansed and brought life to anguished souls, and by the touch of His hand, He healed and gave life to broken bodies. By their faith it was so then, and it is no different now.

That One Year

It's a true principle that God will not do anything to us or for us that is not calculated to benefit us, sometimes even if it has to hurt. The trials of life are, at times, His way of getting our attention and humbling us so that He can teach us.

There was a period of time in my life years ago, when I stubbornly refused to listen to the tiny voice of truth deep in my heart. There was something I knew the Lord wanted me to do, but I refused to admit it. I was the master of rationalizing. I think I even had myself convinced.

Then began a year of my life I will never forget. It started when I went out with some friends to do some sleigh riding behind a team of horses. Eagerly, I jumped onto the sleigh. But when my friend goosed the horses, they began jumping and jerking back and forth instead of pulling together. I was pitched forward off the sleigh and under the horses and bruised up pretty badly. I was sore for a long time.

Shortly after that, I was on my way one morning to take a college final. I was riding a bicycle, when a lady ran a stop sign and hit me. I flew high into the air and landed on my head. After an ambulance ride, the worst headache of my entire life and several hours with a plastic surgeon, my face was sewn back together, and I was released to heal.

It wasn't too long after that, at work one day, when I sliced open my right thumb clear to the bone—another trip to the hospital; more stitches. By now I was getting on a first name basis with the doctor. He took one look at me and said, "Okay, what did you do now?"

The same day I got the stitches out of my right hand, I was told to mount some truck tires, big ones on split-rims. I had heard stories about these huge tires blowing apart and killing people. Well, I didn't want that to happen. So I took what I thought were necessary precautions, which, in the end, only created a bigger problem. With over eighty pounds of pressure inside the tire, it exploded! I will never forget that explosion. The tire and I went into orbit. When I and the dust finally settled back to earth, I had three broken bones, multiple bruises, more scars and stitches than I can recount, and another ambulance ride.

About a month after I finally got my last cast off, I woke up one morning so sick I could not get out of bed. Off to the hospital I went again. This time it was major surgery and several months before I would fully recover. You would think I would have learned and that would be enough, but there was yet one more experience that was mine to have. I then suffered, what seemed at the time, the worst pain of all, a broken heart.

Finally, weak and too exhausted to be stubborn any more, I was ready to wave a white flag. I remember the day when I finally bowed my head in prayer and said, "Heavenly Father, Thy will be done," and for the first time in my life, I meant it.

The entire direction of my life changed that day. Now, many years later, I don't regret a moment of that painful year, only that I waited so long to give in. I am convinced the more total our surrender to Him, the sweeter He will make our joy.

Shaina's Rock

On a recent family camping trip, one of my daughters learned a painful lesson. We came, one afternoon, to a beautiful camping spot along the Snake River. No sooner had we pulled in then my youngest daughter and one of her older sisters took off exploring. As they ran off, I could see a four-year-old girl, a ten-year-old girl, and all these cliffs and monstrous boulders. I may be a doting father, but I was a little concerned. So I warned them.

"Now promise me you won't be climbing around on these slippery rocks."

"Okay, yeah sure, Dad, whatever you say," was the kind of response I got. So I looked at the older girl, and I said again, "Now, please make sure that Shaina stays off those rocks. Okay?"

"I will, Dad."

I knew I couldn't follow them around forever, so I left them and went back to camp. It wasn't too long later my son came running up to me and said in something of a frantic tone, "Dad, Shaina's hurt."

I bailed out of my chair and ran to find her. I met her mother carrying her back to camp cradled in her arms. Even from a distance I could tell she was hurt. She wasn't just crying, she was screaming. I ran and gathered her in my arms. When I looked down at her face, I was nearly sick. Beginning at the bridge of her nose and spreading outward was this horrible swelling and discoloration, and it had just barely happened. I asked them what had happened and was told that when her sister hadn't been with her, she had climbed up on a rock, slipped, fell, and struck her nose.

Her mother and I worked over her for a long time until we were finally able to get her to calm down and determine the extent of the injury. As I held her in my arms and she writhed and screamed in pain, I wanted to scream too. Somehow I felt her pain. I would have done anything at that point to have transferred the injury and pain to myself, or at least have lessened it for her, and I would have done it gladly.

Near the end of the ordeal, as she was finally able to find her voice, she whimpered, "Daddy, I wish I'd never crawled up on that rock."

All I could say was, "I wish you hadn't either, Honey."

I've thought about that since it happened. I wonder if that's what it's like for our Father in Heaven. I know He repeatedly warns us to stay off the rocks, but some of us don't. And, if it brings joy to Him when we repent as the Savior said it does, then, so too, it must tear at His heart when His children suffer. How could it be otherwise?

If you're one of those, like me, who has slipped on the rocks, or even been pushed off by someone else, I invite you not to suffer alone. Return to that Father who was called by John "love," and curl up in the arms of His mercy. Let Him cradle you. Cry unto Him in your hour of pain, and I promise your suffering will last only as long, and be only as painful, as is necessary for your eternal education, and it will then end. He will see to that!

Angie's Solo

The New Year is typically the time of new beginnings. "New Years Resolutions," they're called. Why do we need the start of a new year as an excuse to change, especially when by the second week of January, our resolve so often tends to fade and adds to the blues of an already cold and blue winter season?

I have a friend who grew up in a musical family. They did a lot of singing publicly and privately, but though she sang with her family, Angie had never sung a solo. From childhood, she had always dreamed of doing so, but like so many of us, fear held her back.

Then, in her senior year of high school, she was approached and asked to sing a solo for a church fireside. Feeling inferior and afraid, she was reluctant to accept.

But then the thought entered her mind, "Why not? I've got to start somewhere; what have I got to lose?"

She agreed and began to prepare. The night of her solo came, and it would be an understatement to say she was nervous. A friend approached her and said, "Angie, this is not a performance, but a teaching opportunity. You are only an instrument in the Lord's hands. If you let the spirit take over, the message will be carried to the hearts of those listening."

The power of the Lord's spirit came over her, calming her fears, magnifying her abilities, and filling her with confidence. I was there.

I heard her sing, and it was beautiful; it was powerful and it was touching.

Since that time, Angie has not stopped singing and has been in demand for solo performances. She has been an instrument in the Lord's hands in touching the lives of thousands with His spirit.

It is with Angie, as it is with us. There is a song of many sorts within us all that only needs the power of the Lord's love and spirit to set it free. This new year, if you would be happier, may your first and foremost resolution be to obey the Lord, and thereby, receive the power of His spirit, which will then set the song within you free.

Moses And The Serpent

If men were art, some of them would be masterpieces. Undoubtedly, Moses was one of them. He was one of the greatest prophets who ever lived.

When God came to Moses to call him to lead Israel out of Egypt, Moses' initial reaction was, in effect, "Who, me?"

In response, the Lord assured Moses He would be with him, but still Moses was self-doubting and reluctant. Who can blame him?

Finally, the Lord decided that to demonstrate to Moses was better than to explain, so He said, "What is that in thine hand?"

Moses answered, "A rod."

The Lord then commanded him to "Cast it on the ground." Upon doing so, the stick "became a serpent."

The story continues. It says, "…and Moses fled from before it." It seems Moses was afraid of snakes!

The Lord then said to Moses, "Put forth thine hand, and take it by the tail."

To his everlasting credit, Moses "put forth his hand, and caught it, and it became a rod in his hand."

Through this and other experiences, Moses became the great lawgiver who is revered even today. He was just an ordinary man, until the day God called on him to face what he feared and trust in a higher power. This is faith!

Like Moses, to obey the Lord is to be fashioned by Him into a "masterpiece."

See Exodus 4:1-5.

Chopsticks And Runny Jell-O

One day I came home from work and immediately sensed something funny going on at the house. As the preparations were being made for the evening meal, I noticed some of our finer plates and glasses were on the table, and my wife and daughters were looking at me and pointing at me and speaking in hushed and whispered tones. I'm a little dense, but that looked suspicious.

When we were called to the table, I noticed a fine looking meal of Chow Mien, so far, nothing too out of the ordinary. That is, until my wife announced we were going to eat this meal with chopsticks, no spoons or forks allowed, just chopsticks.

From around the table there came mixed reactions. Some said "All right!" Others were saying, "Oh no!" I won't tell you which one I was. The first few minutes of supper were spent giving chopstick lessons. Since none of us were overly chopstick literate, it was a little like the blind leading the blind. However, it didn't take too long before we began catching on. A growling stomach is a powerful motivator. I'm happy to report it only took me about twice the normal length of time to eat my portion.

One daughter finally gave up and just began to cry, "I just can't do it!"

The ultimate test of skill came when my wife produced jell-o from the fridge that had not completely set up.

Now you have to picture this. There we were, seven hungry people trying every conceivable way to pick up runny jell-o with chopsticks.

My son finally gave up on the chopstick transfer system and just stuck his face on his plate. Me? I waited until everyone was distracted. Then I grabbed my spoon, and using my chopsticks as a plow, I filled my spoon with jell-o, and in three quick bites it was gone.

I can't remember now whether I got full or just so disgusted I gave up. I do remember when I was done eating, my thumb and index finger were stiff and sore from working with the chopsticks. But hey, it was worth it! It was a great family memory.

Sometimes in life we are tempted to throw out the old conventional ways of doing things and try something new. In many instances, that's a good thing to do because it pulls us out of our ruts and brings zest and adventure back to life. When it comes to moral standards and the commandments of God, none of us have lived long enough or grown smart enough to throw out the combined wisdom of the centuries and the omniscience of God. In other words, finding lasting happiness while breaking the commandments of God is as difficult as eating runny watermelon jell-o with chopsticks.

"Folks," to quote a friend of mine, "it just ain't gonna happen!"

A Smile At A Stoplight

It had been a long day. I'd been up since 2:30 a.m., and was just rolling to a stop at the light next to a line of cars. I chanced to look at the car next to me and looked right into the innocent face of a beautiful little girl about three or four years of age. To my surprise, she smiled at me with a gorgeous, wide toothy smile. It was so irresistible I smiled back. And then, to my total amazement, she blew me a kiss!

I didn't know this little girl or her mother who was driving the car. There I was, driving an old beat up, mustard yellow pickup that had long ago seen better days. My clothes were filthy; my hair was a mop; I had on dark sunglasses and sat with one arm propped out the window with a sour expression on my face, and she blows me a kiss?

I was so startled I looked away. As the light changed and the cars began to move, I chanced one more peek at my new friend, and sure enough, there she was, still looking right at me. In a kind of a shy little girl way, she was still smiling the same beautiful smile. Oh, she melted my heart.

I drove away from that stoplight with a different attitude. She changed my day entirely. She warmed my heart and cheered my soul.

If I could only keep that day in my memory and follow that little girl's example, I would refrain from judging people by how they appear. I would love them for what they are, and like her, so warmly let them know it.

Little girl, wherever you are, whoever you are, thanks again for brightening my day and being my teacher.

Wiring Telephones

Once, while doing some remodel work, I accidentally cut my telephone wire. It had to be repaired. The problem was that the area was too small for me to get into it. I couldn't fit. So I asked my twelve-year-old daughter if she wanted to learn to wire a telephone. She gave me that look like, "Right, Dad!" But dubiously agreed to help me. I showed her what to do, gave her detailed instructions, and up the ladder she went.

I turned my attention to hanging a door. A few minutes later she was back standing at my side.

"Oh man, Dad. That's hard!"

She complained for a few minutes. I encouraged her, and she went back up the ladder. It wasn't long before she was back again. "Oh, this hurts," she said, working the soreness out of her shoulders and showing me where a staple was scratching her arm.

I smiled, I sympathized, and I sent her back up the ladder, explaining if she couldn't fix it, I would have to cut a big hole in the wall to repair the damage I'd done.

Over the next thirty minutes or so, she must have come down the ladder four or five more times, each time more frustrated and in more pain. Finally, with only a little bit left to go, she broke one of the wires she had already spliced, leaving a little tiny stub so short she could barely get a hold of it. Oh, that was it. She had had it! I knew at that moment, all I had to do was to say, "Oh, don't worry about it, dear, I'll fix it," and she would have walked away, never again to get any closer to a telephone than picking up a receiver.

I didn't want to tell her to walk away. I mean, much of my childhood was failure. For a good part of my life, I believed I was a loser, that I couldn't do anything right. As a father, it was important to me that she not fail. I didn't know what to say. So I told her she should just walk away for a while, go cool off, and come back later. She took me up on that. She went upstairs, pulled on her sweats and did something I had never seen her do before; she went running! She was frustrated.

She came back about an hour later, and with a renewed sense of determination, she scrambled up the ladder, wedged herself in the ceiling, and about fifteen minutes later she was back standing at my side.

"All done," she announced. In that short time she had accomplished twice as much as before. She was grinning so wide you could have tied it behind her ears.

Now came the real test. Was the phone going to work? She picked up the receiver of the once-dead phone. It worked perfectly!

As we cleaned up, we talked about the experience, and I asked her what she had learned. Among other things she said something that pleased me much.

She said, "Never give up."

We turned to go upstairs. "So how do you feel," I said, "I mean you know, about wiring telephones?"

She looked up at me with a big smile, and she said, "Anybody need a phone wired?"

All Creatures

I enjoy spring very much. It's my favorite time of the year. It seems to me that as the world wakes up from a long winter sleep and springs back to life, it just sort of takes my soul with it.

On one of those first warm days of the season, I couldn't stay inside; I wanted to go outside. So, for a few minutes, I took a group of my students and went out on the front step of the building. On a whim, I asked them to gather in close and sing a-capella the hymn, "All Creatures of Our God and King."

Oh, they could sing! A beautiful spirit descended upon the little group. They sang in praise and rejoicing of the masterful hand of the master creator. It was powerful; it affected me. As they sang, two squirrels nearby began to romp and play and chase each other. One of them ran practically under our feet, with no fear. It was almost like they understood us and were celebrating with us.

As my little choir finished, they were subdued and reverent. I asked them to close their eyes and turn and face the rising sun. They did so, and we all felt the warmth on our cheeks. It felt so good! I asked them then to turn to the north and feel the gentle caress of a slight breeze. They did. I then asked them to be still and listen to the birds singing in the nearby trees. They did.

I don't know how to describe it, but we felt something wonderful; something heavenly. I declared to them if they ever want to see the hand of God, they have only to look carefully at His creations. All the earth bears witness in powerful and unmistakable ways of the hand of its creator, especially at this time of year.

There is a God. I know there's a God because I have climbed and stood on the high mountains; I've watched the sun rise and set; I've seen the lightning flash and heard the thunder roll; I've sat in a meadow and studied wildflowers. He's there, and this earth is His gift!

The Switch

A few days ago, I was in a hurry to get somewhere, when I was caught by a train. Slowly, that thing rolled to a stop directly across my path. A man jumped off and walked a few yards ahead to a switch. He grabbed the lever, and he moved this little tiny section of rail just a few inches, thus enabling the train to move to a different track and change directions.

Now, think about that for a minute. Because of these insignificant things called switches, huge trains, weighing thousands of tons, and being over a mile long are able to radically change directions and end up at completely different destinations.

So it is with people. The tiniest of influences and decisions can cause the most radical of changes in people's lives, leading them to totally different destinations and different courses.

Many years ago, I was asked to give a church lesson to my friends and college roommates. I suppose that may seem harmless enough, except it had only been a matter of weeks for me that I had even begun to consider the existence of God, let alone teach someone else about Him.

I was eighteen-years-old. I knew nothing about God; I wasn't even sure I believed in Him. Never in my life to that point had I taught any kind of a lesson, nor given any manner of a public speech. I didn't have the slightest idea what to say or do. Needless to say, I was scared to death!

Someone thrust a teaching manual in my hands and said, "Here, just follow this!"

Oh, yeah, as if it were that easy.

So I did.

There we were, all my friends and roommates gathered in my apartment on Monday night to hear pitiful little me expound "the mysteries of the kingdom." I began as the manual told me. It came to a place where I was instructed to ask my "audience" a question. So I did, but no one answered. They just sat there looking at the floor. I waited, and I waited.

Finally, in frustration, I blurted out, "C'mon you guys, answer me!"

They looked so shocked, but they answered me; they came to life, all of them! In a matter of minutes, a marvelous gospel discussion ensued. Looking back, I'm sure I just smiled and nodded and had no clue what they were talking about.

When the lesson was over, a number of them came up to me and complimented me on the wonderful lesson "I" had taught. It might seem like a silly thing, but that had a profound impact on me. It was the first time in my life I could remember feeling like I was actually good at something. I believed what they told me.

Because of that experience, I always accepted teaching opportunities that came my way. Eventually, I became a professional teacher and speaker.

The influence of the tiniest compliment switched the entire course and destination of my life. I will always be grateful to those wonderful friends.

Lord, I Believe

I have come to the conclusion that parenting is hard! You know, children don't come with instruction books, but they sure do come with some of the most perplexing problems imaginable. Therefore, I believe to conscientiously raise a child to maturity is to unknowingly, yet inevitably, raise oneself closer to divinity.

While the Savior is on the Mount of Transfiguration with Peter, James, and John, his other apostles are in the valley below waiting for Him. A man who has a son possessed by an evil spirit comes seeking the Master. Since the Master is not present, the disciples attempt to cast out the foul spirit. Because of their lack of faith, they fail. When Jesus comes on the scene, He asks that the son be brought to Him, whereupon the evil spirit in the young man throws him to the ground, and he wallows, foams, and thrashes.

The Master asks the father how long he's been like this. The father replies, "since he was a child. And many times, the evil spirit has tried to destroy him." Then, pitifully, the father pleads, "but if thou canst do anything, have compassion on us and help us."

Did this man have faith? Yes, enough to come and ask for help, but it's obvious from what he says, not enough to have complete confidence in the Master's power.

The Savior, discerning the man's heart and need, says, "If thou canst believe, all things are possible to him that believeth."

Immediately, the father cries out with desperate tears what I consider to be the prayer of the ages. He says, "Lord, I believe, help thou mine unbelief."

In other words, this father is saying, "Lord, I need thy help. I have no place left to go. I have faith you can help me, but it's not enough to save my son. Please give me more."

The Savior answered the prayer, healed the son and restored him whole to his father. I can only imagine the father's rejoicing.

It is no different now. Is there any prayer a loving Father would be more inclined to hear and answer than that of a desperate pleading parent?

Parents, we don't need to do this alone, not the raising of our children. In this world today, we can't afford to. God has not relinquished His Fatherhood just because He's granted us custodial care. His love for them and His ability to help them is greater than ours. And I believe, most of the time He's on our side. It has been aptly said that "one cannot raise Heaven's child without Heaven's help." May the Lord so bless us.

See Matthew 17, Mark 9, and Luke 9.

Lunar Eclipse

One evening, I came home and heard my youngest daughter say something about an eclipse. I hadn't heard much about it. I hurried outside, and sure enough, there was only a small sliver of bright light left.

I'm not an astronomer, but I understand this phenomenon was caused by the moon passing through the shadow of the earth, thus blocking the light of the sun. The dark red color on the moon was caused by rays of sunlight bent by the earth's atmosphere.

I called the family out. They looked up and ooh-ed and ah-ed accordingly. Some of us wrapped ourselves up in a large levi quilt and kept watching. We didn't want to miss a thing.

Ever so gradually, the light disappeared. The moon, though still visible, became dark. It fascinated me! Perhaps I'm a simple minded soul, but it fascinated me how God works in His heavens to teach us. I felt such a sense of reverence, I began to sing a hymn about the glory of God and His creations. My daughters joined in. It was kind of fun.

The neighbors came out to see what was going on. I'm sure they thought we were crazy standing out there in the cold, serenading a lunar eclipse.

On its steady course, the moon continued to climb higher in the sky, until finally the light reappeared. It was strange, but you know, the light seemed more beautiful and bright after the eclipse than it did before.

All the creations of God bear witness of Him and of His truth. We are like that moon. We don't generate our own light; we reflect the light which comes from God. There are times, and it happens to all of us, when through our own foolishness and rebellion we block out the light of God that is our source of happiness. It's those times when we need to repent, change our course, and get back into the light.

There are also those times, eclipses if you will, when our infinitely wise Father and Teacher allows the brilliant light to be withdrawn through no fault of ours, like Jesus in Gethsemane. Often these are times of painfully intense testing and growth, vital for us all. Nevertheless, like that eclipsed moon, the sun's light is not totally withdrawn during these times. If we will hold on, and stay the appointed course, allowing God to work His wonders, the light will return. It's not an "if," it's a "when." The light will return, and when it does, it will seem so much more brilliant than ever it did before. Hold on.

The Gentile Woman

Late in the Savior's ministry, hatred against Him had risen to the point where the Jews were trying to kill Him (John 7:1). Rejected by His own, He leaves Israel and goes north into Syria among the gentiles.

Tired and seeking seclusion, He enters a city where a woman identifies Him and cries after Him, "Have mercy on me, O Lord, thou Son of David; my daughter is grievously vexed with a devil" (Matthew 15:22).

The gospel writers point out something interesting about this woman. She was a Canaanite by birth, a Greek by language and custom, and a Syro-Phonecian by nation. In other words, she is a pure gentile, not at all of the blood of Israel (Bruce R McConkie, The Mortal Messiah, Book 3, Salt Lake City, Utah, 1980, p. 10).

Considering this, how does the Master react to her? He ignores her and keeps right on walking. With faith and persistence, she follows and continues to plead for a miracle on behalf of her daughter. After a time, the disciples become somewhat impatient or annoyed with the woman's pleadings. After all, Jesus has granted miracles to gentiles in the past. Why not now?

"Send her away," they say to him, "for she crieth after us" (Matthew 15:23). In other words, "Lord, give her what she wants and get rid of her" (McConkie, p. 10).

He answers them, "I am not sent but unto the lost sheep of the house of Israel" (Matthew 15:24). His mortal ministry was to be among the covenant children of Abraham, and later, through the Holy Ghost, among the gentiles.

The woman then comes directly to the Savior and falls before Him saying, "Lord, help me" (Matthew 15:25).

His answer to her is most intriguing. "It is not meet," He says, "to take the children's bread, and cast it to the dogs" (Mark 7:27).

It may seem harsh that He refers to her as a dog, but when the Savior used the term "dogs," a better translation would be "little dogs" or "pet dogs," if you will (James E. Talmage, Jesus the Christ, Salt Lake City, Deseret Book Co., 1915, p. 329).

It is as though the Savior is saying to this gentile woman, "I am the bread of life. The Father has sent me to feed the chosen people of Abraham's lineage. Now is their time to feast, but your time will come" (McConkie, p 10).

The woman immediately catches His meaning, and to her eternal credit, she is not offended, but responds, "Yes, Lord: yet the dogs under the table eat of the children's crumbs" (Mark 7:28).

So impressed is the Lord with this woman's faith, He commends her and grants her request. "Be it unto thee," He says, "even as thou wilt" (Matthew 15:28).

The woman returns home to find her daughter delivered and lying on her bed.

This story has troubled many people. Seemingly, it portrays the Savior as harsh and rude. Yet, before we pronounce such a judgment, especially without reading the full text, it would be well to consider the scriptural verse just preceding this story. "[Jesus] arose, and went into the borders of Tyre and Sidon, and entered into [a] house" (Mark 7:24), "and would that no man should come unto him. But He could not deny them; for he had compassion upon all men" (JST Mark 7:22-23).

So He did, and still does. Some may actually feel as unworthy as a dog in the presence of the Lord. My dear friends, I bear witness of His compassion, and of a mercy so abundant and tender it still cannot be denied, for you and even for the lowest of us who will repent.

The Widow's Mite

It seems, when we consider the rest of the population of planet Earth and the populations of the past, we now, at the present time, are a wealthy and indulged people. Some would even call us spoiled. Even the poorest among us would be labeled as rich in some areas of the world. With that in mind, consider this story from the last week of the Lord's life.

Jesus stood in the richly furnished courts of the Temple of Herod, and in the midst of heckling opposition, denounced the leaders of the nation for their hypocrisy and selfish wickedness. The Temple, which previously He had called "My House," He now disowned as "Your House." The Lord's public ministry among the Jews was over.

Moving away from the open court of the Temple, Jesus then entered the Court of the Women, where there were thirteen trumpet-shaped chests that comprised the treasury of the Temple. There He sat downcast and in deep sorrow and probably wept. Then, looking up, Jesus saw a poor widow, known as such by her clothing of mourning, come forward and cast two mites into the treasury. Her offering in American coinage would have been less than half a cent.

Immediately, discerning the heart of the situation, Jesus called His disciples to Him and pointed out the deed of the woman, declaring, "Verily I say unto you, that this poor widow hath cast more in, than all they which have cast into the treasury: For all they did cast in of their abundance; but she of her want did cast in all that she had, even all her living."

It is no accident Jesus drew attention to this simple deed at this critical time, the end of His public ministry. A walking object lesson for individuals and nations, this woman taught the selfish wealthy, in simplistic ways, it is not the size of the offering that counts as much as the heart and the sacrifice behind it.

What about us? Is there someone we should visit? Is there a letter we should write, or an offering we should make that we haven't? It is possible that time has, and will yet memorialize those common people who sacrificed in uncommon ways for worthy day-to-day causes.

See Mark 12:41-44 and Luke 21:1-4.

Dawni's Disappointment

For ten weeks Dawni had prepared for this day. It was the school assembly, and it was her first solo performance on the drums. It had been a struggle for her to get to this point. Initially, her father had been against her playing the drums, but he finally relented and said, "Okay" in the face of her tears and determination. But, before she was allowed to study and play the drums, she had been required to study another instrument.

Patiently, therefore, she learned the flute, waiting until the opportunity came to play the instrument that was her heart's first desire—the drums. And now, that day was here. This assembly was even more significant since it was the first one her mother had been able to attend. It was Dawni's big moment. The night before, she had spent so much time on her clothes, and so much time on her hair; she was so prepared and so eager.

The band director gave the cue and started the piece. But when Dawni struck the snare drum, no sound came out. Someone or something had misadjusted the drum, making it completely useless. Well, there was no way the director could stop the piece now, so it went on without her. While the other percussionists performed and shined, Dawni dropped out of her chair, down on the floor, and desperately tried to repair the damaged drum. Frantically she worked, but the piece ended before she could get it fixed.

From the stands, Mother watched it all, knowing her dear daughter was in trouble, but unable to go to her or help her in any way. At the conclusion of the assembly, Dawni walked out of the crowd and directly to her mother, her eyes swimming with hot tears before she even reached her. So long and so hard had she worked, and the moment was irretrievably gone. It hurt—it hurt a lot!

Her mother reached out and took her in her arms and spoke soothingly and comfortingly. Her older sister, who was also there, left her friends behind and came to Dawni's side, put her arms around her, hugged her, and offered love and encouragement. The two sisters only had a moment to talk with Mom before going back to class. As they turned to go, Dawni's sister put her arm around her again and said, "C'mon Dawni, let's go. There's nothing you could've done about it. You did the best you could."

Together they went. Even moments later, when kids began to make fun of Dawni, her sister jumped in, defended her, and stayed by her until she returned to class.

The pain and Dawni's bitter disappointment was not, and is not gone. Even as she told me this story, she cried. The pain will probably always be there. But one thing's for certain, the pain was made more bearable because of those who shared it with her.

The Story Of Easter

Sometime late Friday afternoon nearing 6:00 p.m., the body of the Lord Jesus was laid by His grieving friends in the borrowed tomb of the rich man, Joseph of Arimathea. It would remain there, while His spirit labored elsewhere, until the predawn hours of Sunday morning.

Matthew records, "[Then] came Mary Magdalene and the other Mary to see the sepulcher.

"And, behold, there was a great earthquake: for the angel of the Lord descended from heaven, and…rolled back the stone from the door, and sat upon it.

"His countenance was like lightning, and his raiment white as snow:

"And for fear of him the keepers did shake, and become as dead men.

"And the angel answered and said unto the women, Fear not ye: for I know that ye seek Jesus, which was crucified.

"He is not here: for He is risen" (Matthew 28:1-6).

Were there ever more momentous words spoken than those? I think not. The resurrection of the Lord, as the capstone of His atonement, is the greatest, most miraculous and significant event of all history.

From the apostle John, "But Mary stood without at the sepulcher weeping: and as she wept, she stooped down, and looked into the sepulcher, "and seeth two angels in white sitting, the one at the head, and the other at the feet, where the body of Jesus had lain.

"And they say unto her, Woman, why weepest thou? She saith unto them, Because they have taken away [the body of] my Lord, and I know not where they have laid Him.

"And when she had thus said, she turned herself back, and saw Jesus standing, and knew not that it was Jesus.

"Jesus saith unto her, Woman, why weepest thou? Whom seeketh thou? She, supposing him to be the gardener, saith unto him, Sir, if thou hast borne him hence, tell me where thou hast laid Him, and I will take him away.

"Jesus saith unto her, Mary." Oh, she recognized the voice! "She turned herself, and saith unto him, Rabboni; which is to say, Master.

"Jesus saith unto her," as she obviously came to embrace him, "Touch me not; for I am not yet ascended to my Father: but go to my brethren, and say unto them, I ascend unto my Father, and [to] your Father; and to my God, and [to] your God" (John 20:11-17).

So significant was the resurrection to the human family, its reality was to be proven to, and attested of, by literally thousands of people. They would see Him, touch Him, and know of an absolute certainty of the reality of the resurrection.

The Judean tomb was empty, and because it was, so shall be yours. As Jesus rose and ascended into the presence of God, so shall you. As He arose in glory and splendor to eternal reward, so shall the faithful. If it were not for that empty tomb, man evermore, and all his possibilities here and hereafter, would be ended in the gloom of misery and death.

Though I might sound a little bit like an Easter Grinch, I would hope instead of bunnies and baskets, and chocolate and new dresses, this is what we would teach the children about Easter, so that their love for the Savior might grow.

Tenderizing

Growing up on a ranch in southeastern Idaho, homegrown beef was an abundant part of our diet, and I liked it, too. But, I remember that some of that beef was tougher than boiled owl. I don't know how old I was, but I well remember walking in the house one day and seeing my mother with this spiked steel mallet thing. She had a raw beefsteak sitting on the cutting board and was just a-beating that steak for all she was worth.

I remember asking her something like, "Mom, what are you doing?"

She explained to me she was tenderizing the meat to make it easier to eat.

"Oh. Well, okay, sounds good to me."

All the years I was at home, I remember my petite little mother beating up beefsteaks.

Lately, I have observed a similar phenomenon going on around me. I've seen students, colleagues, and friends being beat up mercilessly by the trials and difficulties of life. Pounded and beaten, their heads bow and the tears course freely down their cheeks. They are being tenderized. My heart goes out to them, but now they are prepared for the refining and sanctifying fire of the Spirit of God, if they will open themselves to it and receive it.

I recall, when the Savior felt a great need for sustaining strength and guidance, He would often retire to the wilderness and pray.

For example, you'll recall after His baptism, being filled with the spirit of God, Jesus went deep into the wilderness, and for forty days there among the wild beasts, He fasted, prayed, and prepared Himself for His glorious ministry.

On another occasion, on the eve of His calling of the twelve apostles, feeling the need for His father's presence, the Master, "went out into a mountain to pray, and continued all night in prayer to God" (Luke 6:12).

And finally, who can forget that in the depth of the Master's suffering in Gethsemane, He set the example for us all. In the seclusion and peace of a grove of olive trees, a place He often went to be alone, the weight of the world's sins pressed down upon Him. He prostrated Himself upon the ground, "And being in an agony he prayed more earnestly" (Luke 22:44).

And so should we.

Sarah And The Angels

My friend Sarah is a single mom struggling to raise two children while going to college full time. Her day usually begins at 5:00 a.m. with scriptures, prayer, and daily exercise. After getting her babes off to school, she then has her own one-hour commute to college.

One week near the semester's end, the same week her daughter Abi was having her eighth birthday party, Sarah found herself with one of those weeks—an extra load of homework, research papers, and two tests to study for. And then, as if that wasn't enough, she was asked to speak in Church.

On the day of Abi's birthday, Abi got sick, very sick, and had to stay home from school. As the week drew on, Abi did not get better. One night in the middle of the night, Abi cried out in distress for her mother. A blessing was needed, but there was no one to give one. So Sarah prayed, and Abi slept soundly the rest of the night.

The next morning, Sarah began to feel sick as well. Mothers simply cannot afford to get sick. Sarah fasted, prayed and pushed on, feeling more and more physically and emotionally drained. By late Saturday night, sore throat and exhaustion notwithstanding, Sarah put the girls to bed and poured herself into writing a talk she'd been preparing all week, but just wouldn't come.

Somewhere around midnight, Sarah went to bed, planning to get up at 4:00 a.m. and finish the talk. During the night, her younger daughter Isabelle awoke and came into Mom's room with a burning fever. Now both of the girls were sick, and Mom too.

Isabelle climbed into bed with Sarah and promptly threw up. Sarah got up, cleaned it up, crawled back in bed, and went back to sleep.

When the alarm went off a short time later at 4:00 a.m., Sarah rolled over and was surprised to see Isabelle wide awake and staring right at her, her eyes as bright and blue as a summer sunrise.

"Mom, who were those two guys?" She asked.

"I...I don't know," Sarah muttered, not quite awake.

Sarah got down on her knees, offered her prayers, and then had the distinct thought that she ought to ask Isabelle about those "two guys."

"What did they look like?" Sarah inquired.

"Humans," came the reply.

"What were they doing?"

As matter-of-fact as a three-year-old can declare, Isabelle said, "Fixing your throat."

Jesus once said to His disciples, "Are not two sparrows sold for a farthing? And one of them shall not fall on the ground without your Father. But the very hairs of your head are all numbered. Fear ye not therefore, ye are of more value than many sparrows" (Matthew 10:29-31).

We are always and perfectly noticed and known by the Father. He loves us and knows us better than we do ourselves. We do not struggle alone!

Oh, and by the way, as for Sarah, she went to church not the least bit sick, and out of that "fixed throat" came a powerful discourse on the Spirit of God.

Road Rage

Matthew 5:44 may very well have the world's cure for road rage. Not only that, but a way to drive in the worst of conditions almost stress-free. Some may feel the Savior's command to "love your enemies" is difficult enough in normal life, but absolutely impossible in heavy traffic.

A friend of mine was traveling down the Interstate from Idaho to Provo, Utah. As she drove, she began to ponder what it would be like to love all men as the Savior commanded. Her thoughts were particularly relevant since she was traveling through one of Utah's most infamous construction zones, with its equally infamous traffic. It's a stretch of highway where road rage takes on a whole new dimension.

Suddenly, an idea came to her. Rather than looking at each passing car and thinking, "Stupid driver," or some other such unkind thing, she would look at them and say in her mind as they went by, "I love you."

Accordingly, when the next car passed her, she looked over at the driver and said in her mind, "I love you."

As she kept doing it, it actually became fun. All the way from Kaysville on the north to Provo on the south, she told every driver that passed, "I love you."

The remarkable thing about this experience was the more she said it, the more she really felt it. The usual tension and grumpiness that comes with heavy traffic in close quarters melted away! Instead, she felt the kind of peace and joy that comes to all those who love as the Savior loves.

When my friend finally got to Provo, there wasn't the usual huge sigh of relief as she exited the freeway. She was actually having fun; she didn't want the trip to end. When she walked in to greet her family, the feeling went with her, and it even intensified. At that moment, she loved all men, even Utah drivers, with a pure love. The warmth of that love lingered for days and left her yearning for its return.

I have been asked how we can come to love people. I have pondered that question deeply, and this is my answer, just do it!

Consider what kind of world we would have if every driver, every parent, and every person stopped listening to their fears and started listening to their hearts.

We love those we serve, we love those we pray for, and we love most when we give rather than take. In other words, love begins in our actions and moves from there to our heart.

Clifford In Spanish

One day I felt kind of brave and took five active, boisterous children to the public library to check out books. They no more than got in the door then they scattered to all parts of the library to get what they wanted. I wasn't there to check out any books. I only went along to prevent general destruction of the library and harassment of the patrons. After each of them had checked out the books they wanted, and after I had broken up one game of tag and a wrestling match, we went home with our treasures.

Later that evening, one of my daughters approached me and asked me to read a book to her.

"I'll read it to you tonight when we go to bed," I said.

"Okay," she replied.

Late that evening after prayers, my daughter climbed into bed, and I sat down by her to read a story. I read her first book—no problem. I read her second book—no problem. Then I picked up the third book she had checked out, and much to my surprise, my daughter had checked out a book about Clifford the dog—in Spanish. I don't speak Spanish; I can barely speak English.

As I sat there, somewhat bewildered, staring at the book, my daughter said, "C'mon, Dad, read it."

"I can't, Honey."

"Why not?"

"Because it is in Spanish."

Her answer was a classic, "So?"

How do you explain to a five-year-old about language barriers? I couldn't; I didn't know how. Besides that, she insisted I read it. So, I did what any other intelligent father would have done. I looked at the pictures, and in as confident a voice as I could, I made up my own story.

I thought about that experience even as I was sitting by her bed after she'd fallen asleep. What if that book had been the scriptures and not Clifford? What if she had asked me a question about the scriptures, and I didn't know what to answer? What am I going to say?

"I'm sorry, Honey, I don't speak scripture."

How can I help lead my children to their Heavenly Father and His Son if I have to make up my own stories when I look at the scriptures—especially when there aren't any pictures?

Max And Joyce

October 11, 1997, dawned a typical Saturday morning for Joyce. As she went for an early morning walk, her thoughts were of how happy and blessed she was. She thought of Max, her beloved husband, how much they had grown together and how the last few years had been the happiest of her life.

As the day progressed, Joyce became involved in the normal Saturday jobs. Max was across the state attending an education conference and would be back late that afternoon. She was excited to have him home.

However, around 3:45 that afternoon the doorbell rang. When Joyce came to the door, she was met by four close friends and a city police officer. The most awful feeling came over her. She asked them to tell her what she already knew. They explained Max had been killed in an accident that afternoon.

Joyce said, "My worst nightmare was real. At first I didn't think I had heard right. How could that be? Things like this didn't happen to me, but...but to someone else. I remember crying," she said, "until no more tears would come."

Calls went out, and family and friends gathered. Finally, that night, sometime after 1:00 a.m., after they had finally made contact with all the family, Joyce went to bed, but not to sleep. She tossed, turned, cried and wondered if she would just wake up and this would all be an awful dream.

Then, sometime just before dawn, a very special thing happened. Max came to her. She didn't see him; she didn't have to. He was there; she sensed his presence.

Max had never been a very good singer, but he did have three favorite songs, one of which was the great anthem of the pioneers, "Come, Come Ye Saints." A feeling of love and peace came over Joyce as she heard or felt Max sing, "Why should we mourn or think our lot is hard? 'Tis not so. All is right."

And so it was. Somehow she was given to know that he was happy, that it hadn't been his choice to leave. She also knew he didn't want to come back.

Since that sad day, the saddest of her life, Joyce has never felt closer to her Savior, and Max's presence has been with members of the family several times, administering much needed comfort.

Not long ago, as my family was gathered one evening, we got into a discussion about the second coming of Christ. My older children were peppering me with questions about it, and they were hard. Suddenly, my six-year-old daughter, Hannah, who was sitting on my lap, and who I suppose was just a little bored with the present topic, reached up and grabbed my head and pulled it down where she could speak in my ear.

"Daddy," she said, "when you die, will you be my guardian angel?"

Well, it took a minute for me to answer. As I did so, a wonderful feeling came over me.

"Honey," I said, "there's no place I'd rather be."

Why Bad Things Happen To Good People

In my occupation I often hear questions like these: "Why do bad things happen to good people?" "Why is life so unfair?" The hardest of all these questions, "If God really loved us, how could He let this happen?"

I don't know all the answers, but maybe this story will lend some comfort.

Late one evening, years ago, my youngest daughter was toddling around in the kitchen. She was at that awkward stage where she was walking, but not all too steadily. I was upstairs getting ready for bed and my wife was somewhere in the house. All the children were in bed, except for little Shaina.

Suddenly I heard a thump and a terrible cry. I ran downstairs and found Shaina lying on the kitchen floor screaming. Evidently, she had crawled up on a counter chair and fallen off face first onto the floor. When I scooped her up, her face was covered with blood. I ran for the bathroom, and in moments, realized we were going to have to take her to the hospital.

When we got there, the doctor examined the wound and told us if it was not stitched back together, it would leave a horrible, ugly scar. I remember putting our tiny daughter on the table, but when the doctor began to operate on her, her whimpering cries turned into panicked screams. We had no choice. We had to strap her to the table and place her head in restraints. Still, that was not enough. She screamed and thrashed wildly. Finally, the doctor looked at me and told me I was going to have to sit down and hold her head still.

I remember I sat down near her head, and put a hand on each side of her head, and forcefully held it still while the doctor gently and expertly stitched her lip back together. I will never forget her screams and her cries, but most of all, I will never forget those accusing eyes that stared up at me and seemed to say, "Daddy, how could you do this to me? Let me go!" It tore my heart to do that to her, but I did not let her go. The doctor finished, and the wound healed with only a minor scar.

Shaina has been terrified of doctors and hospitals ever since. I'm not sure she's even forgiven me for that night. From her perspective, all she could see was her father inflicting horrible pain and torment on her. From my perspective, the pain was only a temporary thing, and very much worth the end result. Shaina may not see it now, but later, when she matures and her perspective is changed, she'll see it then. I daresay, given the same circumstances, she would even do the same for her children.

Once, when the Lord's people were suffering greatly from the trials and inequities of life, He said to them, "Be still and know that I am God" (D&C 101:16). Remember, when the children of Israel were trapped against the sea, and it looked as though God had led them into the wilderness to die, Moses stood before them and declared, "Fear ye not, stand still and see the salvation of the Lord" (Exodus 14:13).

The Lord said through Isaiah, "My thoughts are not your thoughts, neither are your ways my ways" (Isaiah 55:8).

Those of you who are suffering, despite how much it may hurt now and make absolutely no sense, there will come a day, if we are faithful, when we will see, understand, and even agree.

Living On The Edge

One night, my daughter, Sherise, and I were walking side-by-side on the boardwalk through Norris Geyser Basin in Yellowstone Park. All around us were the boiling pots of jewel-like water. We'd read the signs telling us the boardwalks were there for our own safety and that we'd better stay on them.

As we strolled along, Sherise suddenly stepped out on the very edge of the boardwalk and began a sort of balanced walking while still holding my hand. Well, I jerked her back into the middle of the boardwalk.

"But, Dad," she protested, "I want to walk on the edge."

I couldn't resist. Seeing an opportunity to teach, I said, "Do you know what that means?"

The look she gave me told me she had no clue what I was talking about. I explained to her that "walking on the edge" is what some people call "living on the edge." It means they're always flirting with danger. They push the limits of safety, seeing just how far they can go and just how much they can get away with.

All the while I'm explaining this, Sherise is still out there dancing on the edge. I could see she'd heard me, but the message hadn't registered. So, while she skipped merrily along, I sidled over, and with a quick jerk of my hip, I bumped her off the boardwalk near one of the hotpots.

"Dad!" She protested indignantly.

She scrambled back up before she got caught walking where the law said she shouldn't. She gave me one of those looks that's hotter than the water she'd been standing by.

When she was back up beside me, this time interestingly enough in the middle of the boardwalk, I said, "Now, why shouldn't we walk on the edge?"

"'Cause you might fall off," she said.

"Now, do you understand?" I asked.

She nodded her head, and for the rest of the trip, I never again caught her walking on the edge. And, for the rest of her life, I hope I never do.

Whether we're speaking of our physical safety or our spiritual health, it is the same. Walking or living on the edge is dumb and dangerous. It wouldn't be so bad if Satan weren't walking right by us, but he is. He's just waiting for us to get out on the edge.

Don't be fooled. Satan's not a guy in a red suit with little horns and an attitude. He's real! His hatred is real, and his vigilant opposition is constant. If we live on the edge, sooner or later, and it's not an "if," it's a "when," he will push us off into forbidden territory. I assure you, the pain and effort it takes to get back on, once we're off, is just not worth the risk or the thrill.

For those who find themselves already off the boardwalk and trying to get back on, thank God we have a Savior with an out-stretched hand.

Emmeline

One brisk October morning, Emmeline, her sister MaryAnn, and her younger brother Nathan were in the family van on their way to school. As they rounded a corner, Emmeline was momentarily blinded by the rising sun. She had scarcely begun to press on the brakes, when the sun suddenly vanished behind a truck.

At nearly fifty miles per hour, the van slammed into the back of a slow-moving semi. The horrendous force of the impact drove the dashboard into the front seats, breaking both of MaryAnn's legs. The restraining lap belt seriously injured Nathan in the back seat. Emmeline regained consciousness and realized what had happened. Her first thoughts were of her brother and sister and that she had killed them. Panic ripped through her. Crying and screaming, she struggled to free herself, but the steering wheel and dash had her hopelessly pinned. Suddenly, Emmeline realized she was not alone as a voice spoke clearly and distinctly in her ear.

"Emmeline, it's okay. You're the one that is hurt the worst. Your brother and sister are fine."

Emmeline screamed, "It hurts! It really hurts, I want out!"

"Emmeline, you have to have patience. This is going to take a long time, but when compared with eternity, it will be only a couple of minutes. Patience."

Emmeline stopped struggling and screaming as a feeling of divine peace and well-being filled her soul. So radically did her demeanor change that rescuers standing nearby panicked; they thought she had died!

Paramedics and rescue crews continued to work quickly to cut MaryAnn and finally Emmeline free of the wrecked vehicle. All the while they worked, Emmeline, in spite of horribly painful injuries, was calm, basking in a divine presence. The presence attended her and comforted her until the time she was taken into surgery, some seven hours later.

The Lord is my Shepherd; I shall not want. He maketh me to lie down in green pastures: he leadeth me beside the still waters. He restoreth my soul: he leadeth me in the paths of righteousness for his name's sake. Yea, though I walk through the valley of the shadow of death, I will fear no evil: for thou art with me; thy rod and thy staff they comfort me. Thou preparest a table before me in the presence of mine enemies: thou anointest my head with oil; my cup runneth over. Surely goodness and mercy shall follow me all the days of my life: and I will dwell in the house of the Lord for ever (Psalms 23).

Hannah Hendee

Wisdom picks her battles in matters of principle and fights them fiercely.

October 16, 1780, A band of three hundred Indians, under the command of a British captain named Horton, moved down the White River near South Royalton, Vermont, capturing, killing, and terrorizing the local inhabitants. The Hendee family was warned of the oncoming mobbers. The father set out to warn others of the danger while Mrs. Hendee took Michael, her seven-year-old son, and a younger daughter and fled into the woods.

As they ran, they came headlong into a band of the mobbers. An Indian stepped from behind a tree, grabbed her son and wrestled him away. She demanded to know what they were going to do with him.

One of them who spoke English replied, "Make a soldier of him."

They dragged the sobbing boy away. Mrs. Hendee made her way toward the road carrying her tiny daughter who was screaming in panicked terror.

As she traveled down the road, surely as heartsick and grief-stricken as any mother could be, she was suddenly filled with a surge of steeled resolve and a fierce determination. They could not, they would not keep her little boy!

She went back and faced Captain Horton. Oblivious to the looming danger, she demanded of him her little boy. Horton responded he could not control the Indians, and it was not his concern what they did anyway.

Angry and indignant, Hannah Hendee said, "You are their commander, and they must, and will obey you. The curse will fall upon you for whatever crime they commit, and all the innocent blood they shall shed will be found in your skirts when the secrets of men's hearts shall be made known, and it will cry for vengeance upon your head!"

Her son was brought in. Hannah grabbed his hand and refused to let go. One of the men standing nearby grabbed her son and jerked him away from her, threatening her with a cutlass. Defiantly, she faced him and grabbed the boy again, telling them she would follow them every stop of the way to Canada if she had to. She would never give up; they would not have her son.

This was a unique and singular confrontation. A lone, determined mother fighting for that which she loved and cherished against a mob of bloodthirsty, unprincipled men.

How does the story end? Later that day, the British soldiers and the Indians set out on their march with their captives. Hannah Hendee left camp and crossed the river for home. But when she did, it was with her daughter, Michael her son, and eight other little boys she had rescued from a sure and certain death.

Has this kind of will to fight died in America today? No, I think not. Is there a need to be roused to fight today? There is! For what should we be roused to fight? For our God, our religion, our freedom, our peace, our wives, our children, and our families. Lord help us that we may be roused to fight!

Adapted from Evelyn Wood Lovejoy, History of Royalton, Vermont, (Burlington, Vermont, Free Press Printing Company, 1911) cited in The Spirit of America, Bookcraft Inc. Salt Lake City, Utah, 1998, pp. 43-46.

Courtney's Second Chance

Courtney loves music. She plays the piano and the flute; she sings; she composes; she can do it all. She's wonderfully talented. In a state high school solo competition she won top honors her sophomore and junior year playing the flute. For a high school musician, the state solos are the pinnacles of achievement. To win is to be the best in the state in a highly competitive discipline.

Courtney's senior year arrived. She prepared longer and harder than ever before for her solo. Winning the state solo competition again would be a dream come true. Confident, but a little nervous, she faces the judge in the preliminaries. If she does well here, she goes to state. Now the judge gives the signal, and Courtney begins to play. Suddenly, she makes a little mistake, then another one, then another one!

At that point, the judge lowers her head and begins writing. This makes Courtney even more nervous, and she makes more mistakes, until finally her concentration is completely gone, and it's all she can do to keep from breaking down and crying. She finishes the piece and walks out holding back the tears and knowing in her heart her chances of going to state are gone, permanently!

"I wouldn't go to state," she said, "and I wouldn't get a second chance."

Courtney walked home very slowly that day reliving, as we so often do, over and over those terrible mistakes that had cost her so dearly.

"Oh, how I longed for a chance to prove myself," she said, "to show the judge I really could do it, that I really was worthy of going to state." But there was no way, not now. Her little mistakes, in a weak moment, had irretrievably cost her the opportunity of a lifetime.

That night, as Courtney continued to ponder on the day's events, a thought suddenly struck her. With the judge there was no second chance, but with God there always is.

"If we make a mistake in this life," she said, "our chance to return to our Father in Heaven is not lost. We have a "second chance." We have a chance to prove ourselves to the judge of heaven that we can pass the test. If we make a mistake, we have the opportunity to make it so it doesn't count against us. It will be forgotten."

As these thoughts passed through her mind, the Spirit of the Lord passed through her soul. Peace and power overshadowed the pain of the day's disappointment. That night as she went to bed, it wasn't the agonizing memory of failure that filled my young friend's mind, it was a deeper love and a more profound gratitude for the Lord Jesus Christ, the eternal God of "the second chance."

Enos

One morning, I was helping my children get off to school, and I noticed they weren't listening to me. Several times, I reminded them of various family rules, only to have to turn around and remind them again just a few minutes later. Is there some sort of teenage disorder called "parentally induced selective deafness" or something that makes them unable to hear me? I know I wasn't like that as a kid! Well, if this sounds at all familiar to you, I would like to share a story that gives me hope, that maybe, just maybe, I'm not wasting my breath.

There was a young man who grew up in a good home. His parents were faithful people who made a conscientious effort to see to the proper teaching and training of their children. This young man heard what his parents said; he listened. But as is so typical of youth, he heard with his ears but not with his heart. He didn't fully understand the importance of what he heard, and like so many youth, he made mistakes in his life that left him with the acute pain of guilt.

One day, while he was out on a hunting trip, his mind, probably sparked by the beautiful surroundings he was in, turned from the hunting of animals to the hunting of something else, peace and self-respect. It was as though he looked at himself in the mirror, soul and all, and didn't like what he saw. Guilt and self-loathing swept over him. There had to be more to life than this. At that point, a powerful sense of yearning, a hungering many times more painful than a missed breakfast gnawed at his soul.

It came into his mind what his father had so often taught him about the happiness and peace that comes to the faithful, both in this world and in the world to come. Suddenly, more than anything else in the world, he wanted that happiness. He wanted to know for himself what his dad had taught. He wanted to change, to be a better person, to be forgiven of his sins and have this terrible burden of guilt lifted from him. What he did next is what he had seen his parents do hundreds of times. He dropped to his knees and began to pray; not the routine kind of prayer so common at bedtimes and mealtimes, it was real prayer. It was mighty prayer. The kind of prayer so filled with reaching and sincerity, its power lifts the heart and mind of the offerer from this fallen world to a perfect one. His whole soul was reaching to God.

The voice of the Lord came into his mind and spoke peace to his soul. His sins were forgiven, and by the miracle of Christ, his guilt was swept away. Once more, the cycle of the ages was complete, where the child discovers for himself the wisdom, the power, and the rightness of his parents' oft-repeated words.

This young man's name was Enos. Enos became a prophet and gave the rest of his life to the service of God, thanks to his parents.

Parents, with all the love and power of your heart, teach truth, over and over again if that is what it takes. Some day, when that hungering moment comes for your children, they will know where to turn for nourishment and what to do.

See Enos.

The Flagpole

My son was searching for an Eagle Project to complete the requirements for his Eagle Scout Award. After some searching and connecting with the right people, he decided to build and install a flagpole at a friend's place of employment.

He worked hard, as did others, fulfilling the required forty hours just in the preliminary work of obtaining the materials and preparing them for installation. Some very generous and kind people helped him. Then, just days before he was to put it in, he received a phone call telling him the project was off. His friend had received instructions that no flagpole was to be put in for any reason.

Jed had a real problem. The materials were bought, and he had substantial donations of time, money, and effort, most of which was unreturnable. What was he going to do? A flagpole and nowhere to put it.

Well, he went to work harder. For ten weeks both of us looked for somewhere else to install the pole. We explored every option we could think of, all to no avail; nothing panned out. Finally, on a Saturday in mid-March, our last option fell through.

That night, as Jed went to bed, he knelt to pray and asked the Lord to help him with his Eagle Project. Later that same night, as I went to bed, I also asked the Lord for help.

The next morning at church, I was helping in the nursery with the children as was Scott, one of Jed's scout leaders, when Cheryl, a friend, walked in. She struck up a conversation with Scott about various things, and then suddenly, out of nowhere, she said something like this to him:

"Scott, I need someone to do an Eagle Scout Project. I need someone to put in a flagpole for me where I work."

Scott looked at her like, "You have got to be putting me on." But when he realized she was serious, he jumped on it immediately, made the appropriate connections, and my son was off once more and running.

Call it what you will, but the whole thing is very interesting to me. That was the first time Cheryl had ever been in the nursery, she had no previous knowledge of Jed's predicament, and that very same week she sold her home and moved from the area.

Some may say it was just a coincidence, and that's fine if they do. As for me and my son, we believe in Heavenly Father. I believe He hears and answers the prayers of fifteen-year-old scouts whose backs are against the wall. I believe He hears the concerns of parents who want their children to succeed. Most of all, I believe He loves us.

Isn't there sufficient reason in your life right now that you and He could have a serious conversation?

Mama's Boys

Long ago, in a far away ancient land, a terrible war raged between two mighty armies. An innumerable army of evil invaders had taken many cities. The defenders struggled day and night on many fronts to maintain the cities they had and to reclaim those which they had lost, but they were too few and spread too thin. However, Heaven justified their cause because they were unlike the invaders who fought for power, land, and conquest. The defenders fought in defense of their families, their freedom, their rights, their liberty, and their religion.

Treachery and treason among the ranks of the defenders had cost them dearly and weakened their strength when they needed it most. They were now in desperate circumstances, so desperate it seemed that they might lose all, when, from out of obscurity, came a small band of youth numbering some two thousand. They armed themselves with weapons of war, a covenant to fight to the death, and mighty faith in God. So armed and much needed, they set out and joined forces with their brothers on the southern front.

A plan was devised in which the boys would pass near the fortifications of the strongest army of the enemy to decoy them out. According to the plan, the boys passed the city of the enemy. The bloodthirsty invaders poured forth against them sensing an easy victory. The boys began to run, pretending to be scared, which caused the enemy to pursue with great vigor. The balance of the defenders fell in behind the duped invaders between them and their stronghold.

The plan was for the main army of defenders to catch the invaders from behind, outside of their fortifications, and defeat them on open field battle. But it went awry; the invaders perceived the trap and sped their march after the boys and away from the main army. If the boys turned back, they'd be turning back to certain death. So they marched on, staying just out of reach of the enemy.

On the third day, the pursuing invaders suddenly stopped, leaving the small band of boys uncertain whether they were being lured into a trap, or if their fellow defenders had caught their pursuers from behind. They didn't know.

With faith in their God that they would be delivered from whatever might happen, they turned back, only to discover the two great armies were locked indeed in mortal struggle. Alas, it was their friends who were giving way, not the enemy. With fury and power born of faith in the living God, they threw themselves at the enemy, causing the entire army of the invaders to turn upon the small heroic band of boys. But, they stood firm! Their fellow-defenders rallied, and the army of the invaders, frightened by the ferocity of a group of boys, was surrounded and compelled to surrender. The victory was won. The strongest army of the invaders in that part of the land was defeated.

The great miracle of this ancient battle was that not one of those boys fell among the thousands of dead and wounded on both sides. All stood! All lived! And all would fight again! In large measure, that band of boys was responsible for saving the freedom of their country.

What of those boys? Where did they learn such faith, such undaunted firmness against evil? In their own words they said, "We do not doubt our mothers knew it" (Alma 56:48).

So is the power of a mother, and never was it needed more than now.

See Alma 56

#

October fourteenth is a day Ruth will never forget. Her father, while on his way to work, was killed in an accident. Ruth was eleven years old at the time. The ensuing days of the viewing and funeral were like a nightmare for her.

For weeks, she struggled to grasp that her father was gone, that she couldn't go to him, she couldn't help him. In her anguish, there was no one she could talk to. Her sister seemed so strong; her mother seemed so fragile. She felt if either of them knew her pain, it would destroy them. For a time, Ruth took to walking to the cemetery to her dad's grave, where she would cry and talk to him and find a measure of comfort.

At the beginning, Ruth believed somehow it was her fault her father was gone. After a time, she came to believe her father had abandoned her and the family. Bitter anger and resentment filled her. She could not explain it nor control it. She loved and missed her father, yet at the same time, she came to resent all he stood for and began to rebel against the teachings and standards to which he had devoted his life. So confusing and conflicting did her emotions and thoughts become that it was easier to run from them than to understand them. The most painful thing to do was to think.

In her escape, Ruth became reckless and extreme, working three jobs, pushing her body in sports beyond safe limits. Her eating habits became irregular and dangerous. No one could get close to her. Everyone was pushed away. Ruth became consumed with anger, rebelling against life, and caring nothing whether she lived or died.

Her family tried, but they could not understand her illogical, unreasonable, and rebellious actions. Ruth's frustration and anger became directed at the one person in this life who tried the most desperately to hang on to her and to help her, her mother. Ruth's most frequently used exit in her house was her own bedroom window.

One night, Ruth did not come home. Her mother went to find her, and it erupted into conflict. Back and forth the argument went. Finally, in caustic defiance, Ruth challenged her mother.

"What are you going to do?"

Her mother stopped suddenly. All the life and fight seemed to go out of her. Her voice dropped to a quiet, low tone and defeatedly she said, "Ruth, you can do what you want, but you can't do anything to make me not love you."

Stunned into silence, Ruth left and went down to her room, her mother's words echoing in her mind. She sat on her bed and pondered. Suddenly, it was as though her eyes were opened.

"What am I doing?" She thought. "Why am I so angry?"

At that moment, Ruth came to realize who had been controlling her life, and it wasn't God. Her anger and her bitterness melted into shame and self-disgust. She didn't want to be angry anymore. She didn't want to fight with her mother. She knew, like never before, that no matter what she did, her mother meant it; she was always going to love her.

As Ruth saw herself in her miserable and wretched state, she was filled with a desire to change, to become a better person, to be more kind to her mother. But, how could she change what she herself could not understand? It was then she remembered what she had known as a little child. The Gospel was true, and there was indeed a loving God, a loving Father who could help.

She fell to her knees right there by her bed and begged God to help her, vowing she would give anything to change and to have the feeling she had once felt in Primary. She determined Satan would no longer control her, she was on Heavenly Father's side, whether He wanted her or not. Whatever it took, she would live worthy of the love of her mother.

There was a calmness and a peace that came over her, as she spoke the words and she drifted off to sleep.

Ruth said, "From that moment on, He changed me. Everything with the Gospel tasted good after that. Everything changed. There was no more fighting; there was no more rebelling."

Speaking of her family, Ruth continued, "I don't know why they didn't just give up on me and send me away. Where would I be if they had? I am so happy. I love my mom."

Turn To Pray

I was recently taught something in the scriptures that deeply affected me.

It begins with a question: Where did the Savior go immediately after His baptism and just before the ministry that would end with His life?

Answer: He went out into the wilderness to fast and to pray for forty days in closest communion with His Father.

Another question: Where was the Master on the eve of that crucial day, when His most trusted friends and associates, who would be with Him in His ministry, namely the twelve apostles, were to be chosen and ordained?

Answer: The Savior was on a Galilean mountain, where He spent the better part of the night in prayer with His Father.

And again, where did the Savior with a troubled heart turn when the multitudes misunderstood Him and tried to make Him king against His will?

He went to the mountains. As before, He spent the better part of the night in prayer with His Father.

When the missionaries came back, the missionaries He had sent out, when they returned rejoicing in their great success and the miracles they'd seen, what was the Master's reaction to their rejoicings?

"In that hour Jesus rejoiced in spirit, and said, I thank thee, O Father, Lord of heaven and earth, that thou hast hid these things from the wise and prudent and hast revealed them unto babes" (Luke 10:21). Interestingly, He rejoices in prayer with them.

Lastly, in those monumental moments of Gethsemane, when the fate of all humanity hung in the balance, Jesus is in the deepest agony of any mortal ever known, where does He turn for strength?

He turns where He has always turned, to His Father. "Abba, Father, all things are possible unto thee; take away this cup from me: nevertheless, [not my will, but thine be done]" (Mark 14:36).

"And being in an agony," Luke records, "he prayed more earnestly: and His sweat was as it were great drops of blood falling down to the ground" (Luke 22:44).

Recently, as part of my weekly Church assignment, I was tending the little children in the nursery. Down on my hands and knees, I was having a wonderful time with them when the door suddenly opened. I turned and looked, and there stood tiny little Luke, not yet two-years-old, with his Daddy not a step behind him.

I called to him, "Hi, Luke!"

He took one look at that strange ugly creature on the floor, spun about, and buried his face in his father's knees desperately clinging to him for protection.

Luke reacted instinctively to what he considered a threat. He turned to the surest security he knew, his father.

Where do we turn? Where do we turn when we're happy? Where do we turn when we're sad? Where do we turn when we need strength or council? Don't turn to the world. I pray our relationship with our Heavenly Father will be so close, so constant, and so personal, that it is our deepest nature and first impulse to turn to Him, and only Him, in all our moments of need.

Peace

Twenty years ago I seldom heard the word "stress." Now it seems I hear it everyday from young and old alike. Are we a stressed-out generation? Is the pace of our lives destroying the peace of our lives?

One night, at the Savior's command, the Apostles took ship and with Him, set across the Sea of Galilee. Being weary, Jesus went to the stern of the boat and was soon asleep.

An unusually violent storm arose, blowing down from the surrounding mountains. Huge waves broke over the boat filling it with water, until it was on the verge of sinking.

The disciples were terrified. Coming to the Master, they awoke Him saying, "Master, carest thou not that we perish?"

The Savior arose immediately and rebuked the wind and sea saying, "Peace, be still!" Instantly, the wind abated and there followed a great calm. The disciples were astonished at Him. They knew He had power, but because their fear had over-ruled their faith, they failed to comprehend how far-reaching His power actually was.

For us, if He can calm an angry sea, surely He can calm a troubled heart. He is the one and only source of lasting peace. So much is He the giver of this great gift that Isaiah calls Him the "Prince of Peace," a prince to whom we ought to be subjects at any sacrifice.

See Mark 4:35-39

Change

I am convinced almost anyone can change. The purpose of life is to change. The sacrifice of the Savior insured that. To me, no character in the scriptures exemplifies change more than the Apostle Peter.

Three times, on the night of the Savior's betrayal, Peter denied Him. This, after publicly proclaiming he would never forsake Him. The record says, after the third denial, the cock crowed, and Peter went out and wept bitterly (Matthew 26:75).

I can only imagine the depth of Peter's pain and guilt at what he had done. Surely it must have been one of the lowest points of his life. I've often wondered what thoughts filled his mind during those three days Jesus was in the tomb. Could it have been something such as, "There's no hope for me now; I can never be forgiven. My sin is too great; I've sinned too much. How could He ever love me again?"

If the story of Peter's life had ended there, it would have been a tragedy indeed. But it didn't. On the day of the resurrection, Peter was privileged with a personal visit from the Risen Lord, face to face, one on one. Peter was forgiven and once more encircled in the arms of the Savior's love. It changed him. That change is dramatically illustrated by an event that occurred some two months later.

Late one afternoon, Peter and John walked into the Temple. As they passed through the gate called "Beautiful," a man crippled from birth begged alms of them.

"Look on us," Peter commanded.

The man looked at them expecting to receive something of them, but Peter said, "Silver and gold have I none; but such as I have give I thee. In the name of Jesus Christ of Nazareth rise up and walk."

Peter reached down and lifted the man to stand on feet that had never borne weight. "Walking, [and] leaping, and praising God" the healed man entered the Temple rejoicing.

Under the refining hand of the Master, Peter's denial became the catalyst for his change. Eventually, he became like the Master he worshipped, a man of miracles, eventually even a martyr.

I believe Peter is a pattern for all those who want to change. Whether we are now in the rock bottom of bitter tears and regret for past mistakes, or simply stranded on a plateau of complacency, when invited, the Savior comes and will encircle us in the arms of His love. The effect? We are changed; we are never again the same.

See Acts 3.

Peace On Earth

The night the Savior was born, angels sang in the heavens, "Glory to God in the highest, and on earth peace, good will toward men" (Luke 2:14).

Peace! Of all the words the angels could have said to tell us what the birth of a Savior would mean, they said "peace!" The Lord Jesus; He is peace! Christmas is peace! And so it was in another land a long time ago.

The nation was torn apart. Contention and hate filled the land. On one hand, there were those, few in number, who believed in the eminent coming of Jesus Christ; His birth to this earth. On the other hand, there were those, by far the majority, who refused to believe in the words of the prophets and would not accept the coming of Christ. Every sign and miracle that was manifest was explained away by the unbelievers, either as a coincidence, or a lucky guess. Religion came to be seen in the land as a wicked and seditious tradition. The persecution which began as simple, annoyed gossip soon grew into deadly threatenings and violence.

Suddenly, there arose a group of the non-believers who declared the time was past for the Messiah to be born. Their words raged throughout the land like a summer forest fire causing a tremendous uproar. People caught hold of them and joined in. While the people of God held firm in the faith, the wicked plotted their death. A date was set and plans were made to execute the people of God for their belief in the coming of Christ.

Finally, it came to climax. The next day, those who had believed in the ancient traditions of the coming of Christ were to be murdered by their own countrymen. While the wicked prepared to murder, the righteous prayed mightily all that day.

Then, miracle of miracles, that night as the sun went down below the horizon, it didn't get dark. To the utter astonishment of all the people, the land remained as light as though it were mid-day. A new and glorious star arose in the heavens. The people recognized it as the long promised sign of the birth of Christ.

While the faithful rejoiced in their deliverance, the unbelievers fell to the earth in utter astonishment. Fear and the spirit of repentance came upon them.

The next morning, as the sun arose, the light of faith arose with it. All thoughts of murder and contention were swept away by the spirit that filled the hearts of the people. Peace and good will reigned throughout the land.

The day was Christmas. On the other side of the world, He who would be called the Prince of Peace was born of Mary and laid in a manger. Even in His birth, He who would someday be Savior of us all, even as a tiny babe, saved His people.

Of all things, Christmas is peace! Christ is peace! Now, as then, all who will let the daystar arise in their hearts will know for themselves the blessing invoked by the angels that first night, "Peace on Earth, good will toward men."

See Helaman 16 and 3 Nephi 1.

The Locksmith

Not long ago some friends and I traveled to another city for a speaking engagement. I remember as we carried our stuff inside to set up, I broke my usual pattern of putting my keys in my suit pocket and dropped them in my book bag instead.

The meeting was fun, and the people were wonderful. When it was over, I picked up my book bag and all of our stuff and carried it out and put it in the van. I noticed as I did, I also loaded a purse belonging to one of the group. As I set the purse down, I thought, "I'd better not leave that thing in the van unlocked." So I stepped back, hit the power locks, and shut the door.

No sooner was the door shut then I grabbed for my pockets. My keys were locked in the van. I tried all the doors and windows. That van might as well have been Fort Knox. With my tools and skills, there was no way I was going to get into that van without breaking a window. Well, I felt kind of foolish. I went back and admitted what I had done. The others just laughed and took it all in stride.

What a predicament! We were miles from home and locked out of our vehicle late in the evening. Worse yet, I didn't personally know anyone in that town who could help me. There happened to be a couple of good-hearted fellows there who took pity on us and began making phone calls. After a number of calls, they managed to reach a man who owned a body and fender shop. I was impressed. He dropped what he was doing and came straight over.

As we sat there and watched, he took out his toolbox and, in less time than it takes for me to tell this story, he had the door open. He made it look so easy, because, for him, it was easy.

When it was all over with, and we were inside of our van, I offered to pay him. He refused. He could have made me feel like an idiot, or that I had greatly inconvenienced him, but he didn't, nor did the others who helped me. A number of them stood by and chatted with us until we loaded up and drove off. I left that town with the neatest feeling towards those wonderful people, especially a kind man, skilled with locks.

Who among us has not locked himself out of the kingdom of heaven by his or her own foolishness? No matter what we did, or said, or tried, there was no way for us to get in. We simply didn't know how. Then along came caring friends, family, or church leaders, who called on the master locksmith in our behalf, and He came. With kindness and gentleness, He unlocked the door of heaven for us. Without the Lord Jesus Christ, we would literally be out in the cold, eternally.

Christ is mighty to save; He is very good at what He does. To those of you who struggle with discouragement and disappointment because you just can't be as good as you want to be, and you feel there's just no hope, I have a word of advice. Step aside, and let the master work.

Forward Momentum

In a way, life is a lot like a radio show. We only have a limited amount of time; it's very valuable, and we need to make the most of it.

When I was just a boy, my dad and I went deer hunting one Saturday. In order to get to where we were going to hunt, we had to travel over a small mountain pass in central Idaho. As we approached the pass, the road became slick with fresh fallen snow. I didn't pay much attention to the snow, that is until we came to a steep banked curve on the pass. The curve turned left and banked away from the mountain

to a steep drop-off. As we went into the curve, the car slid sideways with the back end threatening to slide off the mountain. I remember I was convinced we were going to die. I panicked and yelled for Dad to stop. Strangely, he just grinned—you know that kind of grin that says, "I know something you don't"—and said, "I can't stop."

I thought he was crazy. If we didn't stop, we were going to slide off the mountain back end first and roll forever. He quickly explained as long as he kept the rear wheels going forward, we were less likely to slide off. I still don't think I believed him, that is until just a moment later, when something forced him to stop. Then, even though we had stopped and the brakes were locked up, we slowly began to slide backward toward the edge. Now I really panicked! I remember looking out the back window of the car and all I could see was sky.

Calmly, my dad threw the power again to the rear wheels, and they began to dig, scratch and spin. We stopped sliding. It seemed like it took forever, but gradually we inched our way around the curve, the car straightened up, and we went on our way.

I will be forever grateful to a father who understood a simple principle. Unless there is power applied in the forward direction, we will slide backwards, not stand still.

So it is with life. The road to our heavenly home is slick, steep, and fraught with many perils, and there is no standing still. Either we are going forward, or we are sliding back. The power must be continually applied.

Each time you and I keep the commandments, pray, and search the scriptures, individually or with our families, we throw the power to the wheels once more and move forward. Sometimes its seems like you're only moving inches if you're moving at all, and you wonder if it's worth the battle and the opposition. But I promise you, if you persist in these righteous things, as my dad saved me, by the grace of God, you'll save yourself and your family.

Gethsemane

After all the stories we've told, there yet remains one story more important than any other. The Savior's atonement in the Garden of Gethsemane. It is a story that needs to be heard and understood by anyone who has ever wrestled with the bitterness of guilt and the blush of shame, by anyone who has ever felt burdened and inadequate, by anyone who has ever felt worthless and alone, and by anyone who has ever felt life had no purpose and was not worth living.

After the singing of a hymn, Jesus and the Twelve Apostles left the upper room of the last supper and made their way out of Jerusalem to the Mount of Olives. Taking Peter, James, and John, Jesus enters the Garden of Gethsemane, a place where olives were grown and then crushed under intense pressure to extract their life-sustaining oil.

Jesus invites the three apostles to "tarry...and watch" (Mark 14:34). He then goes about a stone's throw away and collapses face-first to the ground praying, "O my Father, if it be possible, let this cup pass from me: nevertheless not as I will, but as thou wilt" (Matthew 26:39). After some time in prayer, Jesus returns to the three apostles, and interestingly enough, they are asleep. Jesus wakes them saying, "What, could ye not watch with me one hour? Watch and pray that ye enter not into temptation" (Matthew 26:40-41).

Jesus leaves them again, and in incomprehensible physical and spiritual agony, brought on by the sins of all mankind and the onslaught of all Hell itself, He bows beneath the load and prays, "O my Father, if this cup may not pass away from me, except I drink it, thy will be done" (Matthew 26:42).

Luke records, "There appeared unto Him an angel from heaven, strengthening him. And being in an agony he prayed more earnestly: and his sweat was as it were great drops of blood falling down to the ground" (Luke 22:43-44).

When He returns the third time, the apostles are again asleep. Shortly, Judas comes and betrays the Master with a kiss. Jesus is then arrested, and with a rope around His neck, is led away eventually to the cross where His atoning sacrifice is completed.

The Savior took upon Him in that garden the sins, pains, sicknesses, and infirmities of His people. His atonement was an infinite burden of sin of an endless stream of individuals (Merrill J Bateman). For that moment in time, He who knew no sin and guilt became for us the greatest sinner of them all. Truly, He is our compassionate high priest who cannot "be touched with the feeling of our infirmities" (Hebrews 4:15).

He understands us and can help us as no one else can. By virtue of His precious blood shed from every pore of His body, He stands between us and justice, pleading our cause eternally.

The Atonement of Jesus Christ is not a legend of long ago and far away. It is a vital truth, an active principle so intimate and intertwined with our daily existence, even now we would fall in profound gratitude if we had even a mustard seed of a glimpse.

This sacred story should, more than anything, help the hopeless and overwhelmed have hope. Millions can testify of His infinite help. Therefore, "Let us...come boldly unto the throne of grace, that we may obtain mercy, and find grace to help in time of need" (Hebrews 4:16).

Index

Discouragement 122, 179, 181

E

Earth 26, 122, 181

Easter 50, 64, 84, 140

Endure 100, 124

Eternal 22, 27, 43, 58, 76, 77, 86, 106, 117, 122, 135, 141, 161, 181

Eternity 28, 33, 42, 43, 83, 156

Example 2, 19, 36, 62, 94, 111, 122, 181

F

Faith 13, 14, 16, 22, 39, 60, 72, 76, 88, 122, 141, 153, 162, 166, 177, 181

Family 28, 38, 40, 42, 122, 181
  Father 2, 3, 19, 38, 44, 48, 54, 65, 76, 87, 100, 116, 124, 130, 138, 142, 149, 153, 158, 162, 168, 172, 181
  Mother 13, 16, 17, 28, 56, 57, 80, 84, 96, 104, 116, 123, 138, 142, 144, 158, 159, 167, 168, 169, 170

Fellowshipping 87

Foolishness 4, 77, 132, 179

Forgiveness 13, 16, 17, 28, 39, 44, 56, 57, 80, 84, 87, 96, 104, 116, 123, 138, 142, 144, 158, 159, 167, 168, 169, 170

Freedom 13, 16, 17, 28, 56, 57, 80, 84, 96, 104, 116, 123, 138, 142, 144, 158, 159, 167, 168, 169, 170

Friends 13, 16, 17, 28, 56, 57, 80, 84, 96, 104, 116, 123, 138, 142, 144, 158, 159, 167, 168, 169, 170

G

Gethsemane 7, 13, 16, 17, 28, 56, 57, 80, 84, 96, 104, 116, 123, 138, 142, 144, 158, 159, 167, 168, 169, 170, 171

God's Love 44, 110

God's Will 114

Golgotha 7, 13, 16, 17, 28, 56, 57, 80, 84, 96, 104, 116, 123, 138, 142, 144, 158, 159, 167, 168, 169, 170

Good vs. Evil 52

Guilt 21, 28, 78, 162, 163, 174, 182, 183

Biography

Glenn Rawson is the son of Orson and Janice Rawson. He was born and raised in Idaho and grew up on a ranch. When he was eighteen-years-old, he joined the Church of Jesus Christ of Latter-day Saints. He later served as a missionary in the Iowa, Des Moines Mission. Upon returning, he enrolled at BYU and earned a BS in Wildlife and Range Science. He began working for the Church Educational System as a seminary and Institute teacher. Along the way, he earned a Masters degree in Educational Administration.

Since 1995, Glenn has been telling these stories on various radio stations. Currently, he works as writer, producer and host of the Joseph Smith Papers; a weekly television documentary on the life of Joseph Smith. He and his wife, the former Debra Hemsley, have seven children and two grandchildren.

Additional works by Glenn Rawson
In the Midst of Thee Volume 2

These works can be found at www.harmonyriver.com

Affiliates

Glenn Rawson's stories can be heard each Sunday through the following media. All times are in Mountain Standard Time (MST)

Preston, ID.   KACH AM 1340 .... 8:00-9:00 AM

Jerome, ID.   KART AM 1400 .... 5:00-8:00 AM

Twin Falls, ID.   KMVX-MIX-103 FM 102.9 .... 5:00-10:00 AM

Burley, ID.   KBAR AM 1230 .... 7:30-8:30 AM

Montpelier, ID.   KVSI AM 1450 .... 8:00 AM-6:00 PM

Montpelier, ID.   KLCE-K264AD FM 100.7 .... 12:00-5:00 PM

Soda Springs, ID.   KITT FM 100.1 .... 8:00-9:00 AM

Idaho Falls-Pocatello, ID.   KLCE FM 97.3 .... 12:00-5:00 PM

Pocatello, ID.   KLCE-K249CM FM 97.7 .... 12:00-5:00 PM

Freedom-Etna, WY.   KLCE-K249CW FM 97.7 .... 12:00-5:00 PM

Mammoth Hot Springs, WY.   KLCE-K280CS FM 103.9 .... 12:00-5:00 PM

Cokeville, WY.   KLCE-292AO FM 106.3 .... 12:00-5:00 PM

Tremonton, UT.   KNFL AM 1470 .... 6:00 AM-6:00 PM

Salt Lake City, UT.   KBYU FM 89.1 HD-2 .... 8:00 AM-9:30 AM

Ogden, UT.   KOGN AM 1490 .... 6:00 AM-6:00 PM

Heber, UT.   KTMP AM 1340 .... 9:00 AM-2:00 PM

Vernal, Roosevelt, UT.   X-94 – KXRQ FM 94.3 .... 6:00 AM-4:00 PM

St. George, UT.   KWBR FM 105.7 .... 8:00-9:30 AM

Show Low/Snowflake, AZ.   KQAZ – MAJIK 101.7 .... 8:00-11:00 AM

Mesa, AZ: All-American Cable Ch. 97 .... 8:00-9:30 AM

Dish Network Ch. 980 (Satellite) .... 8:00-9:30 AM

www.klce.com: KLCE – 97 .... 12:00-5:00 PM

www.byuradio.org: BYU Radio .... 8:00-9:30 AM

www.kzion.com KZION: .... 12:00-2:30 AM; 7-9:30 AM; 11:00AM-1:30PM

www.kzion.com KZION: .... 2:30-7:30 AM; 2:00-7:00 PM

Programming produced by Carl Watkins
www.soundsofsunday.com

Testimonials

"The Sunday morning I found the Glenn Rawson stories associated with Sounds of the Sabbath was for me an awe inspiring experience. I felt that Mr. Rawson was in my personal presence and talking just to me. His life experiences with his fellow man AND with the Savior Jesus Christ to me are real, personal, and true. He has helped me to come closer to our Savior and want to be in His presence. I have found his first publications both written and on tape a joy to listen to over and over again on all days of the week. I will purchase Volume 2 "In the Midst of Thee" when it becomes available. Thank you, Glenn, for producing beautiful uplifting work."

John Willerton

"I am excited for this book. I bought the book specifically because I LOVED his stories and because I use to do a lot of speaking and they were perfect. The stories told in this book have really touched my life in more ways than one. I have listened to Glenn Rawson for many years and he really brings the spirit into our home. His stories are touching and uplifting. Thank you."

Sara Johnson

"I love the stories every Sunday, they certainly help bring the Spirit into our home along with the music on Sounds of Sunday. When I think about it its quit funny, every time I hear the announcement that Glenn is doing a story I holler through the house, Glenn Rawson moment! Can't wait for volume 2."

Curtis Frame

"Boy! To tell you how these stories have made an impact on me will be pretty difficult! Every Sunday when I wake up, I tune my radio to the Sounds of Sunday station where his stories air. I love to hear them because I always feel picked up. Many times I am so touched that tears come to my eyes! They always seem to be relevant in my life. I especially love the stories that he tells of something about the Savior's life or His teachings, or of His love for each of us. Another part of his stories that have made an impact on me are his patriotic stories or stories of patriots from the early days of our nation's birth.

I am a school teacher and taught US History and I loved how he portrayed the love of country that so many of them had as he shared these stories! If ever there was a person that could tell stories that really settled in your heart and made you think about life, it would be Glen Rawson! I can't wait for Volume 2 to come out!"

Joan Souza

"I'm delighted to hear that more of Glenn's great stories are coming into print! Before I found the first volume, I was aiming toward getting an email or phone contact so I could plead with him to publish those great story-lessons I love to hear on Sundays. Not one of them should be lost! I'm so grateful to have a day when I can hear uplifting music during all my house and car time. I was so happy when I found the AM station (can't remember the numbers; it was KOSY-related) where I could hear hymns and gospel songs all week long--and then after a short time away from radio, it was changed! I didn't want talk like I was hearing, just music. However, Glenn's "talks" are just right—short, perfectly expressed, thought-provoking, touching, even humorous, and right on the mark. I'm a writer and proofreader, and I'm picky! Thanks so much for bringing out a new collection of goodness—I'll be watching for it!"

Rosalyn Ostler

"I am so excited for volume 2!!! I have volume 1 and I have used it in several lessons I've given in Young Women and in a few talks in sacrament meeting. I listen to 106.5 in the mornings getting ready for church and I look so forward to hearing Glenn's stories. I make sure I don't have my eye makeup on until after the stories though. Throughout my life I have been touched and taught tremendously by the spirit mostly through music and now also through Glenn's stories. I have related to a few of His stories and am looking forward to reading and hearing more."

Camille

"I am so excited to have Volume 2 coming out. I was so excited when the first one came that I promptly ordered a book for each of my 6 children to have and use in their homes plus the one for me. That is one of the first places that I go when I have a talk, etc. Thanks!!!!"

LaNada Cheshire

"I would love to get a new book of Glenn Rawson's stories. I ordered several copies last time I saw that they were available, and didn't save one for myself. I have friends that are not even religious that listen to the "Sounds of Sunday" just to hear his stories. Thank you, Glenn Rawson."

Lucy Simmons

"Every Sunday morning I look forward to hearing the simple profound stories by Glenn Rawson, they seem to bring meaning and a bit of hope to my life. It helps me know that my Heavenly Father is always watching and gently pushing me. 'We have the Right to Pursue Happiness, But it's OUR Choice to Grasp it!' Thank you Glenn Rawson!"

Tyler Lisonbee

"I have bought two of Glenn Rawson's CD's and have been uplifted each time I listen to them; they add to my relaxing, renewing Sabbath activities. I have lent them to friends to enjoy in their cars while traveling. Thank you so much for your words of comfort, hope and uplift on my way through life."

Pat Rogers

"I appreciate the opportunity to tell others how wonderful Glenn Rawson's stories are. I have not heard one that hasn't touched me profoundly. He is a fabulous story writer. I don't know how he does it, except that it is a gift from our Father. I remember Michael McLean saying something to the effect that, "It's not me who wrote these songs. I just got the chance to hear them first." We have such a loving Father, don't we? Thank you Glenn, for sharing with all of us the experiences that you have learned from our wonderfully patient Heavenly Father."

Carol Lee Rosenhan

"We sent "In The Midst of Thee" to our friends in Eastern Canada as a gift. The struggle of the small Branches in Eastern Canada is hard for us here in the US to understand. Maybe a missionary can relate. Our friends read Glenn's stories each morning to work, and each evening coming home. It was really a help for them to get through the tough times living in small Branches of the Church. They loved his stories and continue to read them over and over. Thanks for putting these great messages into print."

Betty A. Roach

"I appreciate this opportunity to share my feelings about Glenn Rawson's stories. I recently purchased "In the Midst of Thee" because I listen to Glenn on the radio every Sunday Morning and have thoroughly enjoyed his stories and have often wanted to have a copy of a story to share with others. His stories are short and to the point and just leave my heart full and start my week off in such a good way. Glenn, Thank you for sharing your sweet spirit and insights with us."

Geniel McDonald

"Thank You, Glenn, for your stories each week. I listen closely each hour at 20 after the hour. Our whole family loves you. We have even used many of your stories for Ward Prayer thoughts and when my Husband was a Bishop of Young Adults. Please don't stop! Thanks."

Kim Hunsaker

"Glenn is a master storyteller. When I hear his special way of delivering a beautiful message, I remember it and relate to it time and time again."

David Arnold

"Glenn Rawson's stories are how I enjoy the spiritual feeling all day long on Sunday's. Some Sunday's I can't get to church and listening to Glenn's stories help me feel like I have listened to a mini Church lesson. It helps me feel the spirit and it also has helped with my kids talks."

Tammy Gephart

"I absolutely love Glenn's talks. They are so spiritually uplifting. He absolutely sets the tone for my Sunday schedule. Excellent! Fantastic! Awesome!"

Nola Norton

"I used to listen to a different radio station. One day I heard this man named Glenn Rawson tell this amazing story. I listened intently. I remember feeling the spirit so strong as he spoke. I continued to hear his stories through out the day, needless to say, every time I would hear Glenn Rawson speak, I would stop what ever I was doing so I could really concentrate and listen to what he always said. My family will only listen to the radio station that we know we can hear Glenn Rawson's stories on. I have used his talks many times in teaching lessons, and when any one in my family has had to speak. I

have found myself laughing, crying, and cold chills up and down my spine. I fill the spirit all the time with Glenn's stories. I LOVE them all."

RuthAnn McOmie

"I love Sundays to come so that I can listen to "Sounds of the Sabbath" and hear Glenn Rawson's comments. They make me think and reflect on the things that are important in my life. To thank my Heavenly Father for all the good and precious things I have been blessed with."

S Smith

"We have been inspired by Brother Rawson's Sunday Messages. They are great and they have been an inspiration to us."

Clinton Kingsford

"We LOVE Glenn's book, "In the Midst of Thee." It's perfect if we need to prepare for a talk, or for teaching lessons. There's always something that will go along with what we need!"

Linda Hale

"Glenn's stories are amazing. They are simple and beautiful. They teach principles in a way that is so easy to understand. I love listening to these stories. Listening to these stories and applying the principles taught has made me a better person."

Misty Shaw